Vocabulary Workshop

Enhanced Edition

The classic program for:

- *developing* and *enhancing* vocabulary resources

- *promoting* more effective communication in today's world

- *improving* vocabulary skills assessed on standardized and/or college-admission tests

By
Jerome Shostak

Sadlier-Oxford

A Division of William H. Sadlier, Inc.
9 Pine Street
New York, NY 10005-1002
1-800-221-5175

Contents

Copyright © 1996 by
Sadlier-Oxford,
A Division of
William H. Sadlier, Inc.

ISBN: 0-8215-0612-9
    456789/987

Home Office: 9 Pine Street
New York, NY 10005-1002
1-800-221-5175

Foreword

For close to five decades VOCABULARY WORKSHOP has been a highly successful tool for guiding and stimulating systematic vocabulary growth for students. It has also been extremely valuable for preparing students to take the types of standardized vocabulary tests commonly used to assess grade placement, competence for graduation, and/or college readiness. The *Enhanced Edition* has faithfully maintained those features that have made the program so beneficial in these two areas, while introducing new elements to keep abreast of changing times and changing standardized-test procedures, particularly the SAT. The features that make VOCABULARY WORKSHOP so valuable include:

Word List
Each book contains 300 or more basic words, selected on the basis of:
- currency in present-day usage
- frequency on recognized vocabulary lists
- applicability to standardized tests
- current grade-placement research

Units
The words in each book are organized around 15 short, stimulating *Units* featuring:
- pronunciation and parts of speech
New!
- definitions—fuller treatment in *Enhanced Edition*
- synonyms and antonyms
- usage—one phrase and two sentences illustrating literal and abstract/figurative uses of each basic word

Reviews
Five *Reviews* highlight and reinforce the work of the units through challenging exercises involving:
New!
- shades of meaning (SAT-type critical-thinking exercise)
- definitions
- synonyms and antonyms
- analogies
- sentence completions
- word families
- more

Cumulative Reviews
Four *Cumulative Reviews* utilize standardized testing techniques to provide ongoing assessment of word mastery, all involving SAT-type critical-thinking skills. Here the exercises revolve around
New!
- shades of meaning
- analogies
- two-word completions

Additional Features
- A *Diagnostic Test* provides ready assessment of student needs at the outset of the term.
- The *Vocabulary of Vocabulary* reviews terms and concepts needed for effective word study.
- The *Final Mastery Test* provides end-of-term assessment of student achievement.
- *Building with Word Roots* introduces the study of etymology.
- *Enhancing Your Vocabulary,* Levels F through H, introduces students to the study of word clusters.
New!
- *Working with Parts of Speech,* Levels F through H, provides further work with word clusters and introduces 45 new words per level.

Ancillary Materials
- An *Answer Key* for each level supplies answers to all materials in the student text.
- A *Series Teacher's Guide* provides a thorough overview of the features in each level, along with practical tips for using them.
- The *Supplementary Testing Program: Cycle One, Cycle Two* provides two complete programs of separate and different testing materials for each level so testing can be varied. A *Combined Answer Key* for each level is also available.
- The SAT-type *TEST PREP Blackline Masters* for each level provide further testing materials designed to help students prepare for SAT-type standardized tests. (Answers are included in each booklet.)
- The *Interactive Audio Pronunciation Program* is also available for each level.

Pronunciation Key

The pronunciation is indicated for every basic word introduced in this book. The symbols used for this purpose, as listed below, are similar to those appearing in most standard dictionaries of recent vintage. The author has consulted a large number of dictionaries for this purpose but has relied primarily on *Webster's Third New International Dictionary* and *The Random House Dictionary of the English Language (Unabridged)*.

There are, of course, many English words for which two (or more) pronunciations are commonly accepted. In virtually all cases where such words occur in this book, the author has sought to make things easier for the student by giving just one pronunciation. The only significant exception occurs when the pronunciation changes in accordance with a shift in the part of speech. Thus we would indicate that *project* in the verb form is pronounced prə 'jekt, and in the noun form, 'präj ekt.

It is believed that these relatively simple pronunciation guides will be readily usable by the student. It should be emphasized, however, that the *best* way to learn the pronunciation of a word is to listen to and imitate an educated speaker.

Vowels	ā	lake	e	stress	ü	loot, new
	a	mat	ī	kn*i*fe	u̇	foot, pull
	â	care	i	s*i*t	ə	rug, broken
	ä	bark, bottle	ō	flow	ər	b*i*rd, bett*er*
	au̇	doubt	ô	all, cord		
	ē	beat, wordy	oi	o*i*l		

Consonants	ch	child, lecture	s	cellar	wh	what
	g	give	sh	shun	y	yearn
	j	gentle, bridge	th	thank	z	is
	ŋ	sing	t͟h	those	zh	measure

All other consonants are sounded as in the alphabet.

Stress   The accent mark *precedes* the syllable receiving the major stress: en 'rich

Parts of Speech	adj.	adjective	int.	interjection	prep.	preposition
	adv.	adverb	n.	noun	v.	verb
			part.	participle		
			pl.	plural		

The Vocabulary of Vocabulary

English is rich in vocabulary that is particularly useful for describing and discussing the use and abuse of words. By mastering technical and quasi-technical terms of this kind, you will equip yourself to deal more clearly and forcefully with many linguistic problems.

We shall consider here only a sampling of such terms. Not a few of the words already studied in the VOCABULARY WORKSHOP program have an application to the "vocabulary of vocabulary."

I. *From the list of words below, choose the one that best completes each of the following sentences and write it in the appropriate space.*

ambiguous	**paradox**	**rationalization**	**syllogism**
data	**precept**	**redundant**	**thesis**
dogma	**premise**	**semantics**	**valid**

1. The study of word meanings and the ways in which they change is called

   _____ .

2. When the meaning of a statement is not clear, or when it may be understood in several different senses, the statement is said to be _____ .

3. The unconscious process of self-justification that most of us indulge in at times is called _____ .

4. An idea or point of view which a person presents and is prepared to defend against objections may be called that person's _____ .

5. _____ are the facts on which an argument is based.

6. An argument of demonstrable truth or soundness is said to be _____ .

7. A statement assumed to be true and from which a conclusion or conclusions can be drawn is a(n) _____ .

8. The form of reasoning consisting of two statements and a conclusion drawn from them is a(n) _____ .

9. A statement in which an excessive number of words is used to express a given idea, or in which unnecessary repetition occurs, is _____ .

10. A belief that is taught as true and is regarded as unquestionable by those who believe in it is called a(n) _____ .

11. A(n) _____ is a statement that may be true or meaningful but seems to say two opposite things.

12. A commandment or direction given as a rule of action or conduct is called a(n)

   _____ .

II. *From the terms listed on page 1, choose the one that is most appropriate for each of the following and write it in the space provided.*

1. This proposal is based on the assumption that the city's population will decline. _____

2. Help Wanted: Young boy to deliver light packages on the fourteenth floor. _____

3. Repeat that statement again, and write it up. _____

4. All men are mortal. Socrates is a man. Therefore, Socrates is mortal. _____

5. If you had only showed faith in me, I would have passed the examination. _____

6. Although the word *politician* means essentially "one who is active in public affairs," it has acquired a bad connotation in current usage. _____

7. The Ten Commandments. _____

8. The observations you made during a series of experiments in physics. _____

9. The main point I hope to prove tonight is that large-scale warfare has become impossible. _____

10. A passenger sleeping in a moving bus is at rest and also in motion. _____

III. *In each of the following sentences, encircle the word in parentheses that most satisfactorily completes the meaning.*

1. We tried to use our own experience as the basis for judging the (**semantics, validity**) of her argument.

2. Since his basic (**precept, premise**) was wrong, all the conclusions which he drew regarding the state of our economy were also wrong.

3. "We note with keen regret that Mr. Random is recovering from a bad fall on the ice," is an example of a(n) (**rationalization, ambiguity**).

4. "Neither a borrower nor a lender be," is an old (**precept, paradox**) that many people still feel to be sound.

5. I disagree completely with your (**syllogism, thesis**) that human beings are essentially unteachable.

6. The scientists collected (**data, dogma**) from a series of experiments in order to test their hypothesis.

7. "No South American nation is a first-rank industrial power. Argentina is a nation of South America. Therefore, Argentina is not a first-rank industrial power." This is an example of a (**rationalization, syllogism**).

8. The speaker asserted that science is based on (**dogmas, redundancies**) no less unprovable than those accepted in the field of religion.

9. Her assertion that she would not have gone to the junior prom even if she had been invited is pure (**rationalization, semantics**).

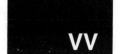

10. His statement was so (**ambiguous, redundant**) that we were able to cut it almost in half without impairing the intended meaning.

11. The long debate over whether the slowdown in business should be called a "depression," a "recession," or a "readjustment" struck me as a futile exercise in (**semantics, syllogism**).

12. "The child is father to the man," is a famous example of a (**dogma, paradox**).

IV. *Explain in your own words what, if anything, is wrong with each of the following statements. The flaw may be due to inept or deficient sentence structure, or to the misuse of words, or to fallacious reasoning, or to ambiguity (deliberate or unintentional). Try to recast all the faulty formulations so that they are rhetorically clear and logically sound. (Use a separate sheet of paper for your answers.)*

1. When the chemists discovered a new type of substance that had never before been known, they knew that it was nylon and not some other synthetic.

2. The two girls were talking to each other. They were leaning out of their windows, on opposite sides of the street. They were unable to agree with each other, because they were arguing from different premises.

3. Nothing is too good for a person like him.

4. The supermarket in our neighborhood specializes in courteous, prompt, and efficient self-service.

5. We are so certain our latest-model coffeemaker will please you that we want you to try it in your home for a week. If you are not completely satisfied, return it to us. So you see, you have everything to lose and nothing to gain.

6. Attention, please! May I please have your attention? A little girl has just been found lost.

7. The salesman called my brother to tell him of a car for sale that won't last long.

8. All seniors belong to the Blue Party. No members of the Blue Party live in Luzerne Heights. We can conclude that no seniors live in Luzerne Heights.

9. All Hindus are pacifists. No Sikhs are Hindus. No Sikhs are pacifists.

10. My cousins live in Woodland Heights. The Morellis live in Woodland Heights. The Morellis must be cousins of mine.

11. Some Canadians are French-speaking. Lawrence is a Canadian. Therefore, Lawrence is French-speaking.

12. The detective trailed the suspect to a hotel, where he made a telephone call.

Diagnostic Test

This test contains a sampling of the words that are to be found in the exercises in this Vocabulary Workshop. It will give you an idea of the types and levels of the words to be studied. When you have completed all the units, the Final Mastery Test at the end of the book will assess what you have learned. By comparing your results on the Final Mastery Test with your results on the Diagnostic Test below, you will be able to judge your progress.

Synonyms   *In the space provided, write the letter of the word or expression that is most nearly the **synonym** of the word in **boldface type** in the introductory phrase.*

1. the **acclamation** of the crowd
a. applause   b. derision   c. indifference   d. criticism

2. dressed with **impeccable** taste
a. vulgar   b. modern   c. faultless   d. strange

3. an **insatiable** appetite
a. temporary   b. shallow   c. limitless   d. informed

4. **germane** to the problem
a. relevant   b. inappropriate   c. indispensable   d. foreign

5. **carping** supervisors
a. cooperative   b. overly critical   c. efficient   d. clumsy

6. respond with **celerity**
a. intelligence   b. satisfaction   c. distrust   d. promptness

7. an **overt** act
a. rebellious   b. obvious   c. nearly fatal   d. habitual

8. spoke with the **distraught** parents
a. strict   b. permissive   c. agitated   d. indifferent

9. a **utopian** community
a. restricted   b. backward   c. idealistic   d. successful

10. tended to **decry** our efforts
a. condemn   b. assist   c. hinder   d. finance

11. a **febrile** imagination
a. inhibited   b. feverish   c. disciplined   d. sentimental

12. **belabor** the point
a. ignore   b. sharpen   c. overwork   d. accept

13. a **prepossessing** smile
a. engaging   b. sarcastic   c. tentative   d. timid

14. **delineate** the character
a. guess   b. portray   c. obscure   d. replace

15. **hallow** the ground on which they fought
a. observe   b. consecrate   c. tread   d. profane

16. received **intermittent** signals
a. interrupted   b. weak   c. clear   d. coded

17. tantamount to a victory
a. equivalent   b. opposed   c. favorable   d. unrelated

18. a **meretricious** display
a. dramatic   b. modest   c. gaudy   d. tasteful

19. used the Faust **motif**
a. theme   b. copyright   c. costume   d. scenery

20. a **sylvan** scene
a. marine   b. horrifying   c. wooded   d. urban

21. jettison the ballast
a. analyze   b. cast off   c. describe   d. conceal

22. allay our fears
a. analyze   b. intensify   c. lessen   d. ridicule

23. a **delectable** dish
a. delightful   b. foreign   c. crude   d. expensive

24. embellish a story
a. confirm   b. adorn   c. ridicule   d. translate

25. attenuated the effect of the measure
a. questioned   b. diluted   c. enhanced   d. reassessed

26. improvident behavior
a. conservative   b. funny   c. mysterious   d. spendthrift

27. a **paucity** of resources
a. dearth   b. variety   c. oversupply   d. sample

28. accuse of **collusion**
a. theft   b. slander   c. conspiracy   d. negligence

29. proffer our apologies
a. present   b. prepare   c. retract   d. reject

30. nothing but a **dilettante**
a. dabbler   b. skeptic   c. thief   d. lout

Antonyms   *Choose the word that is most nearly **opposite** in meaning to the item in **boldface type** in the introductory phrase.*

31. ubiquitous ants
a. scarce   b. omnipresent   c. aggressive   d. bestial

32. a **reputed** mobster
a. fearsome   b. celebrated   c. deceased   d. proven

33. a **defunct** organization
a. profitable   b. ongoing   c. charitable   d. dead

34. a **pejorative** connotation
a. bad   b. colloquial   c. favorable   d. illegal

35. plenary powers
a. absolute   b. limited   c. acute   d. superhuman

36. the **acuity** of her mind
a. dullness   b. flexibility   c. tidiness   d. keenness

37. a **moot** point
a. indisputable   b. pertinent   c. new   d. debatable

38. compose a **panegyric**
a. philippic   b. recipe   c. tribute   d. reply

39. **illusory** gains
a. imaginary   b. actual   c. spectacular   d. supplemental

40. a **testy** reply
a. even-tempered   b. evasive   c. brilliant   d. impatient

41. lend **credence** to a statement
a. support   b. credibility   c. disbelief   d. eloquence

42. the man's **foibles**
a. wealth   b. background   c. children   d. strong suits

43. the **ephemeral** joys of summer
a. long-lasting   b. transitory   c. masculine   d. profound

44. **manifest** an interest in tennis
a. reveal   b. create   c. claim   d. conceal

45. a **hapless** contestant
a. lucky   b. nervous   c. professional   d. brilliant

46. an **obsequious** manner
a. fawning   b. courtly   c. overbearing   d. clumsy

47. **sporadic** precipitation
a. intermittent   b. steady   c. record   d. unseasonable

48. an **abstruse** theory
a. difficult   b. psychological   c. boring   d. straightforward

49. **exhumed** the corpse
a. examined   b. unearthed   c. buried   d. revived

50. a **luminous** explanation
a. new   b. long   c. brief   d. murky

Unit 1

Definitions *From the words in Group A and Group B following, choose the one that most nearly corresponds to each definition below. Write the word in the space at the right of the definition and in the illustrative phrase below it.*

Group A

acquisitive (ə 'kwiz ə tiv)
arrogate ('a rə gāt)
banal (bə 'nal)
belabor (bi 'lā bər)
carping ('kär piŋ)
coherent (kō 'hēr ənt)

congeal (kən 'jēl)
emulate ('em yə lāt)
encomium (en 'kō mē əm)
eschew (es 'chü)
excoriation (ek 'skôr ē ā shən)

1. (*n.*) a formal expression of praise, a lavish tribute _____

the _____ due to the brave

2. (*adj.*) holding or sticking together; making a logical whole; comprehensible, meaningful _____

a(n) _____ explanation

3. (*v.*) to work on excessively; to thrash soundly _____

_____ the obvious

4. (*v.*) to avoid, shun, keep away from _____

_____ bad habits

5. (*adj.*) able to get and to retain ideas or information; concerned with acquiring wealth or property _____

a(n) _____ society

6. (*v.*) to imitate with the intent of equaling or surpassing the model _____

_____ a great writer

7. (*v.*) to claim or take without right _____

_____ royal privileges to themselves

8. (*adj.*) hackneyed, trite, commonplace _____

_____ dialogue

9. (*n.*) a strong denunciation; the act or state of stripping or wearing off the skin _____

a violent _____ of the traitor

10. (*v.*) to change from liquid to solid, thicken; to make inflexible or rigid _____

as the drop of blood slowly _____

11. (*adj.*) tending to find fault, especially in a petty, nasty, or hairsplitting way; (*n.*) petty, nagging criticism _____

the _____ of the critics

8

Group B

germane (jər 'mān)
insatiable (in 'sā shə bəl)
intransigent (in 'tran sə jənt)
invidious (in 'vid ē əs)
largesse (lär 'jes)
ramify ('ram ə fī)

reconnaissance (ri 'kän ə səns)
substantiate (səb 'stan shē āt)
taciturn ('tas ə tərn)
temporize ('tem pə rīz)
tenable ('ten ə bəl)

12. (*v.*) to establish by evidence, prove; to give concrete or substantial form to

_____

unable to _____ the claim

13. (*v.*) to stall or act evasively in order to gain time, avoid a confrontation, or postpone a decision; to compromise

_____

tended to _____ rather than act

14. (*n.*) generosity in giving; lavish or bountiful contributions

_____

the beneficiary of their _____

15. (*adj.*) capable of being held or defended

_____

a(n) _____ theory

16. (*adj.*) so great or demanding that it cannot be satisfied

_____

a(n) _____ appetite for gossip

17. (*n.*) a survey made for military purposes; any kind of preliminary inspection or examination

_____

a(n) _____ in force

18. (*adj.*) relevant, appropriate, apropos

_____

not _____ to the discussion

19. (*v.*) to divide and spread out like branches; to separate into divisions

_____

_____ in all directions

20. (*adj.*) refusing to compromise, irreconcilable

_____

a(n) _____ attitude

21. (*adj.*) habitually silent or quiet, inclined to talk very little

_____

a dour and _____ personality

22. (*adj.*) offensive, hateful; tending to cause bitterness and resentment

_____

a(n) _____ comparison

1

Completing the Sentence *Choose the word for this unit that best completes each of the following sentences. Write it in the space given.*

1. How can we "meet them halfway" when they are so _____ in their opposition to what we propose to do?

2. As a result of recent research, earlier theories about the origin of the universe are no longer considered _____ .

3. Never having any money in one's pockets can be a real trial for someone born with the _____ instincts of a pack rat.

4. I doubt very much that he can _____ his assertion that he won two gold medals in the 1956 Olympics.

5. I would rather work at the most menial, ill paying job than be the recipient of the government's _____ .

6. "There is no need for you to _____ the point," I replied, "when I already understand clearly what your criticism is."

7. Some of the episodes in the series were wonderfully fresh and original; others were just plain _____ .

8. By whose authority did you _____ to yourself the right to decide how the club's money would be spent?

9. Students who seek high grades must learn to _____ the joys of that one-eyed monster, the TV set.

10. In any crisis, the longer a person _____ , the greater the danger is likely to become.

11. The purpose of military _____ remains the same whether cavalry or helicopters are used: to learn as much as possible about the enemy.

12. When the temperature outside dropped suddenly, the water in the ditch _____ into a mass of icy sludge.

13. I don't object to the inclusion of anecdotes in a serious lecture, but they should at the very least be _____ to the subject.

14. The problem of rooting out bigotry and prejudice _____ into virtually every area of our national life.

15. The novel contains an interesting study of a miser's _____ lust for gold and its evil effects on those around him.

16. There is nothing wrong with _____ the great singers of the past as long as you eventually develop a style that is all your own.

17. Even the most severe critics showered _____ on the young writer for the remarkable narrative power of her first novel.

18. Your essay would be a great deal tighter and more _____ if you removed all the extraneous information it now contains.

19. "The victim must have been tied up," the coroner said, "because his wrists and ankles show clear signs of chafing and _____ ."

20. Despite the _____ and nit-picking of a few petty minds, I feel we have substantially improved our local school system of late.

21. In my humble opinion, there is absolutely no justification for making such _____ distinctions between the two types of product.

22. In spite of his size, he was so _____ that we tended to forget that he was even in the room.

Synonyms   *Choose the word for this unit that is most nearly* **the same** *in meaning as each of the following items. Write it in the space given.*

1. a denunciation, castigation; censure   _____

2. to verify, prove, confirm, validate   _____

3. tight-lipped, uncommunicative   _____

4. pertinent, relevant, apropos   _____

5. a tribute, panegyric, eulogy   _____

6. a scouting expedition, survey   _____

7. defensible, justifiable, maintainable   _____

8. to beat into the ground, overwork   _____

9. to expropriate, usurp, commandeer   _____

10. unquenchable, ravenous, voracious   _____

11. stale, trite, hackneyed   _____

12. to hedge, dillydally, procrastinate   _____

13. uncompromising, unyielding, obdurate   _____

14. to harden, jell, coagulate, solidify   _____

15. to steer clear of, shun, avoid   _____

16. to branch out, extend into   _____

17. nit-picking, hairsplitting, caviling   _____

18. generosity, liberality, munificence, bounty   _____

19. connected, unified, consistent, cohesive   _____

20. to copy, imitate, mimic   _____

21. greedy, grasping, avaricious, retentive   _____

22. malicious, spiteful, prejudicial, pejorative   _____

Antonyms   _Choose the word for this unit that is most nearly_ **opposite** _in meaning to each of the following items. Write it in the space given._

1. fresh, novel, original, new   _____

2. stinginess, miserliness, niggardliness   _____

3. indefensible, unjustifiable   _____

4. to melt, liquefy   _____

5. a condemnation, castigation, criticism   _____

6. to embrace, adopt   _____

7. to refute, disprove, invalidate   _____

8. praise; a tribute, panegyric, eulogy   _____

9. muddled, chaotic, disjointed   _____

10. to relinquish, renounce, abdicate, abandon   _____

11. garrulous, loquacious, prolix, verbose   _____

12. complimentary, flattering, ameliorative   _____

13. irrelevant, extraneous, inappropriate   _____

14. to act decisively   _____

15. lukewarm, halfhearted; yielding   _____

16. unconcerned about material possessions or gain, altruistic; unretentive   _____

Choosing the Right Word   _Encircle the_ **boldface** _word that more satisfactorily completes each of the following sentences._

1. The tycoon's business interests (**arrogate, ramify**) in so many directions that she runs the risk of being in competition with herself.

2. When the evidence of his misconduct became irrefutable, he saw that his position was not (**banal, tenable**) and resigned.

3. Your critical comments about my "lack of social background" may be true, but they are not (**coherent, germane**) to my qualifications for office.

4. After the editor read the story, he returned it to the author with only a few (**carping, coherent**) criticisms of minor faults penciled in the margin.

5. Ethelred the Unready was so reluctant to face the Vikings who invaded his kingdom that in effect he (**ramified, temporized**) himself off the throne.

6. "That word has such (**invidious, germane**) connotations in modern American parlance," I said, "that I would hesitate to use it, even in jest."

7. Aristotle had such a(n) (**tenable, acquisitive**) mind that his writings are a veritable gold mine of odd and interesting information.

8. The Constitution is uniquely designed to provide protection against those who might seek to (**substantiate, arrogate**) undue power to themselves.

9. The new batting champion in our softball league is a(n) (**insatiable, taciturn**) young man who prefers to let his bat do his talking for him.

10. What evidence can you offer to (**substantiate, eschew**) the assertion that capital punishment does not deter potential murderers?

11. My purpose is to expose the evils of bigotry—not to (**excoriate, emulate**) a few misguided individuals.

12. After I mowed the lawn for an hour, he gave me a whole dollar with the air of a feudal lord bestowing (**largesse, intransigence**) on a grateful serf.

13. His figure bears witness to his (**acquisitive, insatiable**) appetite for the pleasures of the table.

14. In that moment of grief, the conventional expressions of sympathy I had always considered (**tenable, banal**) were surprisingly comforting.

15. The mood of easy cordiality with which we began the meeting soon (**congealed, temporized**) into icy politeness.

16. The speech was so filled with (**encomiums, reconnaissance**) that I found it hard to believe that the subject of all this acclaim was plain old me.

17. I am proud to have it said of me that I am stubborn and (**invidious, intransigent**) when genuine moral issues are involved.

18. The poor woman was in such a state of shock after the accident that she couldn't give a (**coherent, taciturn**) account of what had happened.

19. Aerial (**reconnaissance, encomium**) of the enemy's positions provided the general with the information he needed to plan his attack.

20. In our attempt to improve the quality of life in America, we should not be too quick to (**eschew, cohere**) old ideas simply because they are old.

21. Suddenly a band of ruffians set upon us and began to (**congeal, belabor**) us with blows and curses.

22. Even a very imperfect human being may sometimes have virtues of mind or character that are worthy of (**carping, emulation**).

Unit 2

Definitions
From the words in Group A and Group B, choose the one that most nearly corresponds to each definition below. Write the word in the space at the right of the definition and in the illustrative phrase below it.

Group A

accost (ə 'käst)
animadversion
  (an ə mad 'vər zhən)
avid ('av id)
brackish ('brak ish)
celerity (sə 'ler ə tē)

covenant ('kəv ə nənt)
devious ('dē vē əs)
gambit ('gam bit)
halcyon ('hal sē ən)
histrionic (his trē 'än ik)
incendiary (in 'sen dē er ē)

1. (*adj.*) desirous of something to the point of greed; intensely eager   _____

    a(n) _____ reader

2. (*n.*) a legendary bird identified with the kingfisher; (*adj.*) of or relating to the halcyon; calm, peaceful; happy, golden; prosperous, affluent   _____

    _____ days

3. (*adj.*) straying or wandering from a straight or direct course, roundabout; done or acting in a shifty or underhanded way   _____

    _____ methods

4. (*v.*) to approach and speak to first   _____

    not afraid to _____ a stranger

5. (*adj.*) deliberately setting or causing fires; designed to start fires; tending to stir up strife or rebellion; (*n.*) one who deliberately starts fires; one who causes strife   _____

    a(n) _____ bomb

6. (*n.*) a comment indicating strong criticism or disapproval   _____

    the _____ of the critics

7. (*n.*) a solemn agreement   _____

    a(n) _____ like the Mayflower Compact

8. (*n.*) in chess, an opening move that involves the risk or sacrifice of a minor piece in order to gain a later advantage; any opening move of this type   _____

    a popular cocktail-party _____

9. (*adj.*) having a salty taste and unpleasant to drink   _____

    _____ water

10. (*adj.*) pertaining to actors and their techniques; theatrical, artificial, melodramatic _____

a(n) _____ speech

11. (*n.*) swiftness, rapidity of motion or action _____

responded with surprising _____

Group B

maelstrom ('māl strəm)	**sacrilege** ('sak rə lij)
myopic (mī 'äp ik)	**summarily** (sə 'mer ə lē)
overt (ō 'vert)	**suppliant** ('səp lē ənt)
pejorative (pə 'jôr ə tiv)	**talisman** ('tal iz mən)
propound (prə 'paúnd)	**undulate** ('ən dyə lāt)
propriety (prə 'prī ə tē)	

12. (*adj.*) asking humbly and earnestly; (*n.*) one who makes a request humbly and earnestly _____

not as a conqueror but as a(n) _____

13. (*v.*) to put forward, offer, suggest for consideration; to set forth _____

_____ a startling new hypothesis

14. (*n.*) the state of being proper, appropriateness; (*pl.*) standards of what is proper or socially acceptable _____

question the _____ of the request

15. (*adj.*) open, not hidden, expressed or revealed in a way that is easily recognized _____

a(n) _____ threat to our security

16. (*v.*) to move in waves or with a wavelike motion; to have a wavelike appearance or form _____

writhe and _____ to the sound of the music

17. (*n.*) improper or disrespectful treatment of something held sacred _____

commit _____

18. (*n.*) an object that serves as a charm or is believed to confer magical powers _____

rabbit's feet and other _____

19. (*adj.*) nearsighted; lacking a broad, realistic view of a situation; lacking foresight or discernment _____

a(n) _____ foreign policy

20. (*adv.*) without delay or formality; briefly, concisely _____

_____ ousted from office

21. (*adj.*) tending to make worse; expressing disapproval
or disparagement _____

a(n) _____ expression

22. (*n.*) a whirlpool of great size and violence; a situation
resembling a whirlpool in violence and destruction _____

caught in the _____ of revolution

**Completing
the Sentence**

*Choose the word for this unit that best completes each
of the following sentences. Write it in the space given.*

1. In the eyes of most Americans, people who burn or spit on our flag are

guilty of an intolerable _____ .

2. In Grandmother's day, standards of _____ required that a
young lady wear a hat and gloves when she went out in public.

3. I stand before you an abject _____ , hoping against hope
for a sign of your forgiveness.

4. During the rainy season, the highway sank at so many points that its

surface began to _____ like the track for a roller coaster.

5. Saying that "people who live in glass houses shouldn't throw stones" is not

an effective response to their _____ on your conduct.

6. Down in the main square, a wrinkled old peasant was selling charms and

_____ to ward off the evil eye.

7. Ever since Darwin first _____ his theories of evolution,
controversy about their validity has raged all over the world.

8. The _____ with which he accepted our invitation to dinner
suggested that he was badly in need of a good meal.

9. As an employee of the local polling service last summer, it was my job to

_____ people on the street and ask their opinions.

10. To our dismay, we discovered that the water we had worked so hard to

bring to the surface was too _____ for human consumption.

11. The Japanese attack on Pearl Harbor was a(n) _____ act of
war that the American government could in no way overlook.

12. My brother is such a(n) _____ collector of toy soldiers that I
sometimes think our house has been invaded by a pint-size army.

13. On the return trip, we cut straight across the meadows rather than take the

more _____ path along the river.

14. The tons of _____ material dropped by enemy aircraft
turned the city into a roaring inferno.

15. To be really convincing on stage, an opera singer must possess both vocal and _____ abilities.

16. His pale face, hunched shoulders, and _____ stare showed that he had spent his life poring over old books and documents.

17. On July 4, 1776, fifty-six men made a historic _____ to devote their lives, fortunes, and honor to creating a new nation.

18. The suffix -*ling* often has a(n) _____ connotation, as in the word *princeling*, derived from *prince*.

19. After the prisoner had been found guilty of treason, he was led before a firing squad and _____ executed.

20. Many a rich Southern planter saw all of his or her financial resources swallowed up in the _____ of the Civil War.

21. We looked back on those _____ years before the war broke out as a kind of "golden age" that would never come again.

22. Any book on chess strategy usually discusses the standard opening moves, such as the "knight's _____ ."

Synonyms *Choose the word for this unit that is most nearly **the same** in meaning as each of the following items. Write the word in the space provided.*

1. a desecration, profanation, defilement _____

2. a charm, amulet _____

3. to propose, put forward, set forth _____

4. a petitioner, suitor _____

5. a whirlpool, vortex; chaos, turbulence _____

6. clear, obvious, manifest, patent _____

7. theatrical, melodramatic, stagy _____

8. nearsighted; shortsighted _____

9. promptly, peremptorily, abruptly _____

10. a ploy, stratagem, ruse, maneuver _____

11. a solemn agreement, pact, compact _____

12. fitness, appropriateness, correctness _____

13. a criticism, rebuke, reproof _____

14. roundabout, indirect; tricky, sly, artful _____

15. salty, briny, saline _____

16. tranquil, serene, placid; palmy _____

17. to ripple, fluctuate, rise and fall _____

18. eager, greedy, keen, enthusiastic _____

19. to buttonhole, approach, confront _____

20. inflammatory, provocative _____

21. promptness, alacrity, speed, rapidity _____

22. disparaging, derogatory, deprecatory _____

Antonyms   *Choose the word for this unit that is most nearly* ***opposite*** *in meaning to each of the following items. Write the word in the space provided.*

1. slowness, sluggishness, dilatoriness _____

2. secret, clandestine, covert, concealed _____

3. farsighted _____

4. praise, a compliment, a pat on the back _____

5. complimentary, ameliorative _____

6. direct, straightforward; open, aboveboard _____

7. unseemliness, inappropriateness _____

8. soothing, quieting; a peacemaker _____

9. reluctant, indifferent, unenthusiastic _____

10. fresh, clear, sweet _____

11. low-keyed, muted, untheatrical, subdued _____

12. to evade, avoid, shun _____

13. turbulent, chaotic, tumultuous _____

Choosing the Right Word   *Encircle the* ***boldface*** *word that more satisfactorily completes each of the following sentences.*

1. He is the kind of person who is concerned not with real moral values but simply with appearances and (**propriety, celerity**).

2. John Masefield's poem "Sea Fever" has a(n) (**propounding, undulating**) rhythm that actually gives one the feeling of being on a rolling ship.

3. "His acts of defiance have been so (**myopic, overt**) and premeditated that I have no choice but to fire him," she said sadly.

4. "I realize that this kind of financial (**gambit, sacrilege**) has its risks," she said, "but I expect it to pay off handsomely in the end."

5. He regarded his Phi Beta Kappa key as a(n) (**talisman, animadversion**) that would open all doors and win him universal acceptance.

6. After years of failure to sell a single story, the young writer described himself bitterly as "a(n) (**pejorative, avid**) collector of rejection slips."

7. Instead of imbibing the (**brackish, suppliant**) waters of superstition, let us refresh ourselves with long drafts of pure, clean common sense.

8. She was buffeted about in a veritable (**gambit, maelstrom**) of emotions, caused mainly by her own dissatisfaction with herself.

9. Nary a ripple disturbed the (**halcyon, brackish**) calm of the sea on that glorious summer's afternoon.

10. In an age when the United States has truly global responsibilities, we can ill afford leaders with (**myopic, pejorative**) points of view.

11. The adoring fan regarded my negative comments about his favorite singer as tantamount to (**maelstrom, sacrilege**).

12. Without even considering the new evidence that I was prepared to present, they (**deviously, summarily**) denied my appeal to reopen the case.

13. I certainly do not claim that my performance in office was beyond criticism, but I deeply resent (**animadversions, covenants**) on my honesty.

14. His methods were so complicated and his purposes so (**avid, devious**) that we were not sure if he was spying on the enemy or on us.

15. Since the word *appeasement* is associated with disastrous concessions to Adolf Hitler, it has acquired a(n) (**pejorative, overt**) connotation.

16. His reckless words had an (**incendiary, overt**) effect on the already excited crowd, and large-scale rioting resulted.

17. Twice in the 20th century, the nations of the world have entered into a (**covenant, talisman**) to cooperate in safeguarding international peace.

18. The infatuated schoolboy, in one of his more restrained expressions, described himself as "a (**sacrilege, suppliant**) at the altar of love."

19. The "tentative explanation" that he (**propounded, accosted**) was ingenious, plausible, and totally wrong.

20. As the defendant left the courtroom, he was (**propounded, accosted**) by a group of reporters seeking his reaction to the verdict.

21. Walt tends to react slowly, but when he feels that his own interests are at stake he can move with striking (**celerity, myopia**).

22. Although all politicians must have some ability to dramatize themselves, it is very easy to overdo the (**proprieties, histrionics**).

Unit 3

Definitions   From the words in Group A and Group B following, choose the one that most nearly corresponds to each definition below. Write the word in the space at the right of the definition and in the illustrative phrase below it.

Group A

articulate (*v.*, är 'tik yə lāt; *adj.*, är 'tik yə lit)
cavort (kə 'vôrt)
credence ('krēd əns)
decry (di 'krī)
derogatory (di 'räg ə tôr ē)

dissemble (di 'sem bəl)
distraught (dis 'trôt)
eulogy ('yü lə jē)
evince (i 'vins)
exhume (eks 'hyüm)
feckless ('fek ləs)

1. (*adj.*) very much agitated or upset as a result of emotion or mental conflict _____

the _____ relatives of the trapped miners

2. (*n.*) belief, mental acceptance _____

give _____ to the report

3. (*adj.*) lacking in spirit and strength; ineffective, weak; irresponsible, unreliable _____

a(n) _____ youth

4. (*v.*) to condemn, express strong disapproval; to officially depreciate _____

_____ bigotry

5. (*v.*) to pronounce distinctly; to express well in words; to connect by a joint or joints; (*adj.*) expressed clearly and forcefully; able to employ language clearly and forcefully; jointed _____

the most _____ speaker in the class

6. (*adj.*) designed to belittle or degrade; disparaging _____

a(n) _____ remark

7. (*v.*) to romp or prance around exuberantly _____

_____ gleefully on the dance floor

8. (*v.*) to disguise or conceal, deliberately give a false impression _____

unable to _____ my feelings

9. (*n.*) a formal statement of commendation; high praise _____

deliver the _____ at the funeral

10. (*v.*) to remove from a grave; to bring to light _____

_____ a body

11. (*v.*) to display clearly, to make evident; to provoke _____

did not _____ any sign of panic

Group B

intractable (in 'trak tə bəl)	**unwonted** (un 'wōn tid)
murky ('mər kē)	**utopian** (yü 'tō pē ən)
nefarious (nə 'fâr ē əs)	**verbiage** ('vər bē ij)
piquant ('pē kənt)	**verdant** ('vər dənt)
primordial (prī 'môr dē əl)	**viscous** ('vis kəs)
propinquity (prō 'piŋ kwə tē)	

12. (*adj.*) green in tint or color; immature in experience or judgment _____

_____ grasslands

13. (*n.*) language that is too wordy or inflated in proportion to the sense or content, wordiness; a manner of expression _____

meaningless _____

14. (*adj.*) dark and gloomy, obscure; lacking in clarity and precision _____

the _____ waters of the lake

15. (*n.*) nearness in place or time; kinship _____

the _____ of the two cities

16. (*adj.*) hard to manage, stubborn, not responsive to discipline _____

a(n) _____ child

17. (*adj.*) stimulating to the taste or mind; spicy, pungent; appealingly provocative _____

a(n) _____ dish

18. (*adj.*) founded upon or involving a visionary view of an ideal world; impractical _____

_____ schemes

19. (*adj.*) wicked, depraved, devoid of moral standards _____

a(n) _____ plot

20. (*adj.*) having a gelatinous or gluey quality, lacking in easy movement or fluidity _____

left a(n) _____ residue in the pan

21. (*adj.*) not usual or expected; not in character _____

answered with _____ spirit

22. (*adj.*) developed or created at the very beginning; going back to the most ancient times or earliest stage; fundamental, basic _____

the _____ forests

3

Completing the Sentence *Choose the word for this unit that best completes each of the following sentences. Write it in the space given.*

1. For as far as the eye could see, _____ fields of unripe corn swayed gently in the morning breeze.

2. How could we draw any clear ideas from a talk that was so disorganized, confused in language, and generally _____ ?

3. Some students are as docile as lambs; others are as _____ as mules.

4. An educated citizenry will not give _____ to wild charges of extremists seeking to undermine our political and economic system.

5. When news of the school fire ran through town, _____ parents rushed to the scene of the blaze.

6. The assembly speaker couldn't be understood because he mumbled his words instead of _____ them clearly.

7. Though diesel fuels are not as thick as motor oil, they are a good deal more _____ than regular gasoline.

8. I have always regarded the man as something of a daredevil, but on this occasion he approached the problem with _____ caution.

9. Since my apartment is in such close _____ to my office, I usually walk to work.

10. When Bill was told that he had made the varsity wrestling team, he began to _____ around the gym like a young colt.

11. The new chairman _____ what she called the "deplorable tendency of so many Americans to try to get something for nothing."

12. In the hands of our hopelessly _____ producer, what should have been a surefire hit turned into a resounding fiasco.

13. The NCAA has in recent years cracked down hard on such _____ practices as "shaving points."

14. Such spices as red pepper make many of the sauces used in Cajun cooking delightfully _____ .

15. Though I prefer to be as open and aboveboard as possible, I have learned that it is sometimes wiser or more tactful to _____ .

16. He clothes his puny ideas in such highfalutin _____ that they resemble gnats in top hats and tails.

17. Sadly, the _____ schemes of high-minded idealists usually founder on the rocks of practical realities.

18. When new evidence turned up in the case, the court ordered the coroner to _____ the victim's body and reexamine it.

19. Every Memorial Day, the Mayor delivers a(n) _____ extolling the selfless devotion of those who have died in defense of this country.

20. You cannot hope to conceal the shortcomings in your own abilities by making _____ remarks about the abilities of others.

21. I believe there is an overall design to the universe that has been visible ever since the first living thing crawled out of the _____ ooze.

22. Even at an early age, my sister _____ a strong interest in studying medicine.

Synonyms   *Choose the word for this unit that is most nearly* **the same** *in meaning as each of the following items. Write it in the space provided.*

1. proximity, nearness; kinship, similarity   _____

2. verbosity, prolixity; diction, jargon   _____

3. feeble, helpless, incompetent, ineffectual   _____

4. green; artless, naive, immature   _____

5. to dissimulate, disguise, mask, feign   _____

6. idealistic, visionary, pie-in-the-sky   _____

7. belief, credit, trust, confidence   _____

8. original, primeval, primal, fundamental   _____

9. agitated, frantic, distracted   _____

10. unusual, uncommon, unexpected, atypical   _____

11. gummy, sticky, thick, gelatinous   _____

12. to pronounce; to elucidate; eloquent   _____

13. dark, dim, obscure, cloudy, unclear   _____

14. to cut capers, prance, gambol, romp   _____

15. wicked, iniquitous, reprehensible   _____

16. pejorative, disparaging   _____

17. to disinter, unearth, uncover   _____

18. to condemn, denounce; to devalue   _____

19. pungent, spicy, tangy, zestful _____

20. unruly, refractory, unmanageable _____

21. to exhibit, evidence, manifest; to occasion _____

22. a panegyric, encomium, tribute, testimonial _____

Antonyms   *Choose the word for this unit that is most nearly* **opposite** *in meaning to each of the following items. Write it in the space provided.*

1. to tout, commend, extol, laud, praise _____

2. bland, insipid, tasteless, mild _____

3. runny, watery, aqueous _____

4. disbelief, skepticism, incredulity _____

5. a philippic, diatribe, invective _____

6. realistic, pragmatic, down-to-earth _____

7. tongue-tied, halting; to mumble, slur _____

8. calm, composed, collected _____

9. competent, capable, effective _____

10. virtuous, honorable; praiseworthy, meritorious _____

11. customary, usual, typical _____

12. complimentary, laudatory _____

13. to bury, inter _____

14. scorched, sere, barren, arid _____

15. remoteness, distance _____

16. clear, transparent, lucid, limpid _____

17. docile, obedient, submissive _____

Choosing the Right Word   *Encircle the* **boldface** *word that more satisfactorily completes each of the following sentences.*

1. His (**viscous, unwonted**) interest in the state of my finances strengthened my suspicions that he was about to ask for a loan.

2. The United States is cooperating with the other nations of the world in an effort to check the (**intractable, nefarious**) trade in narcotics.

3. Far from being unpleasant, her slight foreign accent added an extra dash of spice to her already (**primordial, piquant**) personality.

4. (**Exhumed, Distraught**) with grief, they sat motionless for hours, staring blankly into space.

5. Trying to read your (**viscous, utopian**) prose is just like trying to swim upstream through custard.

6. One of the duties of a President is to (**cavort, articulate**) the policies and programs of his administration in a forceful and convincing way.

7. An accomplished hypocrite usually finds it very easy to (**dissemble, decry**) his or her true feelings as circumstance dictates.

8. Despite all the reports of "miraculous" cures, you would be well advised to withhold (**verbiage, credence**) until the drug has been fully tested.

9. The new Mayor is a curious mixture of the hardheaded pragmatist and the (**utopian, murky**) reformer.

10. The (**credence, propinquity**) of our ideas on handling the problem made it very easy for my colleague and me to produce the report in record time.

11. The book has an interesting plot, but the author has practically smothered it in endless (**verbiage, eulogy**).

12. When life was easy he was all dash and confidence, but in times of trouble his essentially (**piquant, feckless**) character came to the fore.

13. Though the work hadn't seen the light of day for over a century, a daring impresario (**cavorted, exhumed**) and staged it to great public acclaim.

14. The behavior of armies in wartime often evinces the (**murky, primordial**) blood lust that civilized people have not yet fully overcome.

15. After repeated efforts to appeal to his better nature had proved completely fruitless, I decided he was utterly (**derogatory, intractable**).

16. Not surprisingly, the address was a notably evenhanded affair in which the speaker had cleverly mixed (**eulogy, verbiage**) with admonition.

17. From the bridge, the rescue team could just make out the blurred image of a car beneath the (**murky, unwonted**) waters of the river.

18. The investigating committee (**decried, dissembled**) the use of substandard materials and slovenly workmanship in the housing project.

19. Unfortunately, the (**nefarious, verdant**) hopes and aspirations of my youth have been somewhat blighted by the icy blasts of reality.

20. The extraordinary musical talents of Wolfgang Amadeus Mozart (**evinced, dissembled**) themselves at an amazingly early age.

21. The public will not readily accept an intensive investigation designed to turn up (**derogatory, feckless**) information about so popular a figure.

22. From the deck of our luxury liner, we occasionally caught sight of schools of porpoises (**cavorting, evincing**) playfully in the waves.

Review   Units 1–3

Analogies   *In each of the following, encircle the item that best completes the comparison.*

1. brackish is to **salt** as
a. gritty is to oil
b. saccharine is to vinegar
c. piquant is to spice
d. tart is to sugar

2. insatiable is to **satisfy** as
a. indispensable is to use
b. inadvisable is to do
c. incontestible is to prove
d. intractable is to control

3. philanthropist is to **largesse** as
a. saint is to sacrilege
b. skinflint is to parsimony
c. turncoat is to propriety
d. skeptic is to credence

4. usurper is to **arrogate** as
a. navigator is to ramify
b. lawyer is to cavort
c. candidate is to evince
d. impostor is to dissemble

5. scout is to **reconnaissance** as
a. spy is to espionage
b. guide is to sabotage
c. guard is to intelligence
d. trooper is to vigilance

6. summarily is to **celerity** as
a. leisurely is to alacrity
b. rashly is to prudence
c. incidentally is to intention
d. gingerly is to care

7. histrionic is to **acting** as
a. germane is to singing
b. primordial is to weaving
c. choreographic is to dancing
d. utopian is to cooking

8. firebrand is to **incendiary** as
a. fool is to articulate
b. peacemaker is to conciliatory
c. diplomat is to derogatory
d. politician is to invidious

9. distraught is to **composure** as
a. seemly is to propriety
b. giddy is to seriousness
c. pejorative is to realism
d. intransigent is to constancy

10. feckless is to **willpower** as
a. myopic is to depth
b. avid is to enthusiasm
c. overt is to openness
d. nefarious is to cunning

11. bombastic is to **verbiage** as
a. laudatory is to animadversions
b. melodramatic is to histrionics
c. critical is to encomiums
d. illiterate is to talismans

12. glue is to **viscous** as
a. fog is to murky
b. snow is to verdant
c. gloom is to halcyon
d. rain is to feckless

13. suppliant is to **entreaty** as
a. explorer is to covenant
b. surgeon is to credence
c. speculator is to gambit
d. clerk is to propinquity

14. taciturn is to **talk** as
a. carping is to criticize
b. sluggish is to move
c. articulate is to speak
d. shy is to hesitate

15. tenable is to **hold** as
a. audible is to listen
b. edible is to cook
c. visible is to see
d. tangible is to defend

16. acquisitive is to **gain** as
a. devious is to status
b. modest is to glory
c. conceited is to honor
d. mercenary is to profit

17. banal is to **novelty** as
a. bland is to piquancy
b. coherent is to consistency
c. germane is to appropriateness
d. unwonted is to force

18. virtue is to **emulate** as
a. vice is to eschew
b. honor is to excoriate
c. achievement is to decry
d. excess is to temporize

19. club is to **belabor** as
a. ax is to substantiate
b. rope is to congeal
c. pestle is to propound
d. shovel is to exhume

20. wave is to **undulate** as
a. tide is to cascade
b. billow is to recede
c. maelstrom is to swirl
d. pool is to trickle

Identification   *In each of the following groups, encircle the word that is best defined or suggested by the introductory phrase.*

1. what a nitpicker seems always to be doing
a. coherent   b. overt   c. incendiary   d. carping

2. the rate at which gossip travels
a. celerity   b. encomium   c. histrionic   d. devious

3. going back to the time of the first appearance of life on this planet
a. primordial   b. feckless   c. viscous   d. taciturn

4. one who is unwilling to compromise
a. tenable   b. invidious   c. intransigent   d. pejorative

5. improper use of a house of worship
a. suppliant   b. sacrilege   c. animadversion   d. verbiage

6. lavish tips given to waiters, parking lot attendants, etc.
a. eulogy   b. gambit   c. credence   d. largesse

7. how you might properly characterize a cliché
a. piquant   b. insatiable   c. banal   d. halcyon

8. what a person who vacillates would probably do in a crisis
a. cavort   b. temporize   c. propound   d. articulate

9. so nearsighted that one can't see the woods for the trees
a. avid   b. unwonted   c. myopic   d. derogatory

10. rolling hills and lush meadows in springtime
a. verdant   b. brackish   c. intractable   d. summarily

11. "So he came up to me and asked me for a quarter."
a. accost   b. eschew   c. emulate   d. ramify

12. hiding one's disappointment behind a brave smile
a. arrogate   b. congeal   c. dissemble   d. evince

13. will consider only matters directly related to the question under discussion
a. incendiary   b. germane   c. pejorative   d. suppliant

Shades of Meaning   *Read each sentence carefully. Then encircle the item that best completes the statement below the sentence.*

The narrator of Edgar Allan Poe's tale "Descent Into the Maelstrom" tells the harrowing story of his deliverance from a gigantic vortex.   **(2)**

1. In line 1 the word **Maelstrom** most nearly means
a. chaos   c. mine
b. turbulence   d. whirlpool

Fire marshals soon apprehended the incendiary responsible for the conflagration that reduced to smoking embers the historic waterfront hotel. **(2)**

2. The word **incendiary** in line 1 is used to mean
    a. arsonist
    b. rabble-rouser
    c. agitator
    d. criminal

The ultimatum delivered to the besieged American forces at Bastogne in December 1944 is reputed to have evinced the succinct response "Nuts!" **(2)**

3. The best definition for the word **evinced** in line 2 is
    a. displayed   b. demanded   c. provoked   d. exhibited

By decrying the nation's currency, the government hoped to both spur exports and curb inflation. **(2)**

4. The word **decrying** in line 1 is used to mean
    a. denouncing   b. depreciating   c. condemning   d. supporting

Unfortunately, the procurement specifications were framed in technical verbiage that only those thoroughly versed in such matters could understand. **(2)**

5. In line 2 the word **verbiage** most nearly means
    a. prolixity   b. jargon   c. verbosity   d. code

The space vehicle was equipped with an articulated boom designed to deploy and retrieve small satellites and scientific devices. **(2)**

6. The best definition for the word **articulated** in line 1 is
    a. elucidated
    b. state-of-the-art
    c. well-spoken
    d. jointed

Antonyms   *In each of the following groups, encircle the word that is most nearly **opposite** in meaning to the **boldface word** in the introductory phrase.*

1. an **overt** attempt to topple the government
a. concealed   b. obvious   c. humorous   d. unnecessary

2. a **coherent** policy
a. recent   b. disjointed   c. strange   d. workable

3. a **piquant** dish
a. bland   b. foreign   c. expensive   d. spicy

4. a **nefarious** scheme
a. intelligent   b. feasible   c. new   d. meritorious

5. an **intractable** group of students
a. dull   b. diverse   c. docile   d. young

6. a **myopic** point of view
a. sincere   b. scholarly   c. farsighted   d. foolish

7. the **propriety** of your behavior
a. tactfulness   b. correctness   c. morality   d. unseemliness

8. substantiate a claim
a. refute   b. introduce   c. report   d. confirm

9. murky water
a. salty   b. turbulent   c. clear   d. polluted

10. the **propinquity** of the two places
a. remoteness   b. importance   c. size   d. splendor

11. a **tenable** theory
a. scientific   b. indefensible   c. interesting   d. complicated

12. an infuriatingly **tactiturn** person
a. arrogant   b. mean   c. stupid   d. garrulous

13. with their accustomed **largesse**
a. haste   b. rudeness   c. stinginess   d. skill

14. the **animadversions** of the critics
a. raves   b. salaries   c. backgrounds   d. quirks

15. an **avid** reader
a. enthusiastic   b. indifferent   c. quick   d. intelligent

Completing the Sentence

From the following words, choose the one that best completes each of the sentences below. Write the word in the space given.

Group A

invidious	talisman	belabor	gambit
congeal	encomium	summarily	brackish

1. "I do not wish to _____ the point," I replied, "but I feel that I must reiterate my concerns in regard to this proposal."

2. Some baseball players are a bit superstitious and carry around all sorts of charms and _____ to help them in a game.

3. Under some forms of martial law, anyone caught spying for the enemy may be hauled before a firing squad and _____ executed.

4. I did not expect him to support me for class president, but I was hurt by his _____ remarks about my lack of qualifications.

5. As the temperature plummeted during the night, the slush in the street began to _____ into an icy mass.

Group B

emulate	ramify	credence	avid
excoriation	propinquity	covenant	propound

1. When we come to analyze the problem of unemployment, we find that it _____ into many areas of our social structure.

2. To show you that questions of right and wrong are often difficult to decide, I am going to _____ an interesting ethical problem for your consideration.

3. How can you be so naive as to give _____ to claims that obviously have no basis in fact?

4. There are few things young people may do more damaging than trying to _____ someone unworthy of admiration or imitation.

5. In some versions of the story, Faust is ultimately saved from the frightful consequences of the _____ he made with the devil.

Word Families

A. *On the line provided, write a* **noun form** *of each of the following words.*

Example: acquisitive—**acquisitiveness**

1. undulate _____

2. taciturn _____

3. murky _____

4. coherent _____

5. utopian _____

6. articulate _____

7. substantiate _____

8. avid _____

9. piquant _____

10. exhume _____

11. ramify _____

12. histrionic _____

13. emulate _____

14. banal _____

15. myopic _____

16. viscous _____

17. intransigent _____

18. devious _____

19. arrogate _____

B. *On the line provided, write a* **verb** *related to each of the following words.*

Example: acquisitive—**acquire**

1. eulogy _____

2. coherent　　　　　　　　　　　　_____

3. excoriation　　　　　　　　　　_____

4. carping　　　　　　　　　　　　_____

5. animadversion　　　　　　　　_____

6. derogatory　　　　　　　　　　_____

7. suppliant　　　　　　　　　　　_____

8. devious　　　　　　　　　　　　_____

9. insatiable　　　　　　　　　　　_____

10. reconnaissance　　　　　　　_____

**Filling
the Blanks**　　　　*Encircle the pair of words that best complete each of
the following passages.*

1. For what must have been the first and only time in his life, the overly
   cautious general did not _____ or vacillate but committed
   his troops to battle with _____ celerity.
   a. arrogate . . . overt　　　　　　c. carp . . . myopic
   b. temporize . . . unwonted　　　d. dissemble . . . feckless

2. From the top of the mountain that summer afternoon, I looked out on a(n)
   _____ panorama of fields and pasturelands through which
   countless streams and rivulets _____ like so many serpents
   slithering lazily across a carpet.
   a. murky . . . articulated　　　　c. verdant . . . undulated
   b. avid . . . ramified　　　　　　d. primordial . . . cavorted

3. Little did we realize, as we _____ blithely on the beach
   during those _____ and cloudless days of early summer,
   that the world was moving inexorably into the maelstrom of total war.
   a. evinced . . . piquant　　　　　c. emulated . . . insatiable
   b. belabored . . . utopian　　　　d. cavorted . . . halcyon

4. Someone who is by nature as skeptical as I am usually refuses to give any
   _____ to the kinds of wild allegations thrown about in an
   election until they have been _____ by solid evidence.
   a. credence . . . substantiated　　c. largesse . . . exhumed
   b. celerity . . . decried　　　　　　d. propriety . . . propounded

5. Despite the somewhat strident _____ of some professional
   critics and the inane _____ of a few literary pedants, the
   work enjoyed a notable popular success.
   a. encomiums . . . largesse　　　c. animadversions . . . carping
   b. verbiage . . . eulogies　　　　d. excoriations . . . sacrilege

Unit 4

Definitions   *From the words in Group A and Group B following, choose the one that most nearly corresponds to each definition below. Write the word in the space at the right of the definition and in the illustrative phrase below it.*

Group A

asseverate (ə 'sev ə rāt)
atrophy ('a trə fē)
bastion ('bas chən)
concord ('kän kôrd)
consummate (v., 'kän sə māt;
    adj., kən 'səm ət)

disarray (dis ə 'rā)
exigency ('ek sə jən sē)
flotsam ('flät səm)
frenetic (frə 'net ik)
glean (glēn)
grouse (graús)

1. (*adj.*) frenzied, frantic, highly agitated   _____

    a(n) _____ search for the missing report

2. (*n.*) disorder, confusion; (*v.*) to throw into disorder   _____

    in a state of _____

3. (*n.*) the wasting away of a body organ or tissue; any progressive decline or failure; (*v.*) to waste away   _____

    muscles that have begun to _____

4. (*v.*) to affirm earnestly and with emphasis   _____

    _____ their loyalty to the cause

5. (*v.*) to gather bit by bit; to gather small quantities of grain left in a field by the reapers   _____

    eventually _____ the truth

6. (*adj.*) complete or perfect in the highest degree; (*v.*) to bring to a state of completion or perfection   _____

    a work of _____ artistry

7. (*n.*) a type of game bird; a complaint; (*v.*) to complain, grumble   _____

    _____ about one's salary

8. (*n.*) a fortified place, stronghold   _____

    a(n) _____ of conservatism

9. (*n.*, *often pl.*) urgency, pressure; urgent demand, pressing need; an emergency   _____

    the _____ of the situation

10. (*n.*) floating debris; homeless, impoverished people   _____

    _____ and jetsam

11. (*n.*) a state of agreement, harmony; a treaty   _____

    a spirit of _____

Group B

incarcerate (in ′kär sə rāt)	**pecuniary** (pi ′kyü nē er ē)
incumbent (in ′kəm bənt)	**prepossessing** (prē pə ′zes iŋ)
jocular (′jäk yə lər)	**pusillanimous** (pyü sə ′lan ə məs)
ludicrous (′lüd ə krəs)	**recumbent** (ri ′kəm bənt)
mordant (′môr dənt)	**stratagem** (′strat ə jəm)
nettle (′net əl)	

12. (*adj.*) pleasing, tending to create a favorable impression _____

a(n) _____ manner

13. (*adj.*) in a reclining position, lying down, in the posture of one sleeping or resting _____

_____ on the couch

14. (*v.*) to imprison, confine, jail _____

_____ in the state penitentiary

15. (*adj.*) ridiculous, laughable, absurd _____

a(n) _____ comment

16. (*adj.*) biting or caustic in thought, manner, or style; sharply or bitterly harsh _____

a(n) _____ criticism

17. (*adj.*) contemptibly cowardly or mean-spirited _____

a(n) _____ attitude

18. (*n.*) a prickly or stinging plant; (*v.*) to arouse displeasure, impatience, or anger; to vex or irritate severely _____

_____ by the reply

19. (*n.*) a scheme to outwit or deceive an opponent or to gain an end _____

resorted to a clever _____

20. (*adj.*) obligatory, required; (*n.*) one who holds a specific office at the time spoken of _____

a duty _____ on all Americans

21. (*adj.*) consisting of or measured in money; of or related to money _____

_____ considerations

22. (*adj.*) humorous, jesting, jolly, joking _____

in a delightfully _____ mood

4

Completing the Sentence   *Choose the word for this unit that best completes each of the following sentences. Write it in the space given.*

1. Most people regarded the government's attempt to avert a war by buying off the aggressor as not only shameful but _____ as well.

2. The defeated army fled in such _____ that before long it had become little more than a uniformed mob.

3. It was pleasant to see the usually quiet and restrained Mr. Baxter in such a(n) _____ and expansive mood.

4. People who are used to the unhurried atmosphere of a country town often find it hard to cope with the _____ pace of big-city life.

5. There was indeed something _____ about what my father aptly referred to as my sister's "winning" smile.

6. Since I had had only one year of high-school French, my attempts to speak that language on my trip to Paris were pretty _____ .

7. Despite all their highfalutin malarky about helping the poor, I suspect that their interest in the project is purely _____ .

8. Almost every case of muscle or tissue _____ is the result of disease, prolonged disuse, or changes in cell nutrition.

9. The purpose of our _____ was to draw in the safety man so that Tom could get behind him to receive a long pass.

10. The high ground east of the river formed a natural _____ , which we decided to defend with all the forces at our disposal.

11. Shakespeare's Timon of Athens is a disillusioned misanthrope who spends his time hurling _____ barbs at the rest of mankind.

12. As soon as he struck the opening chords of the selection, we realized that we were listening to a(n) _____ master of the piano.

13. I get my best ideas while lying down; the _____ position seems to stimulate my brain.

14. The _____ of my present financial situation demand that I curtail all unnecessary expenses for at least a month.

15. Though next to nothing is known about Homer, historians have been able to _____ a few odd facts about him from studying his works.

16. When he takes the Oath of Office, the President _____ that he will protect and defend the Constitution of the United States.

17. It is _____ on all of us to do whatever we can to help our community overcome this crisis.

18. I regret that Nancy was _____ by my unfavorable review of her short story, but I had to express my opinion honestly.

19. Even critics of our penal system admit that so long as hardened criminals are _____ , they can't commit further crimes.

20. I have yet to meet an adult who did not _____ about the taxes he or she had to pay.

21. The _____ that we observed here and there in the harbor bore mute testimony to the destructive power of the storm.

22. Peace is not just the absence of war but a positive state of _____ among the nations of the world.

Synonyms   *Choose the word for this unit that is most nearly **the same** in meaning as each of the following items. Write it in the space given.*

1. risible, ridiculous, laughable, absurd   _____

2. a ruse, trick, ploy, subterfuge   _____

3. cowardly, craven, lily-livered   _____

4. winsome, engaging, captivating   _____

5. prone, prostrate, supine; inactive   _____

6. to collect, cull, pick up, gather   _____

7. urgency; a need, demand, requirement   _____

8. to clinch, conclude; masterful   _____

9. agreement, unanimity; a pact, covenant   _____

10. to imprison, jail, intern, immure   _____

11. a citadel, stronghold, rampart, bulwark   _____

12. frenzied, frantic   _____

13. floating wreckage, debris   _____

14. obligatory, mandatory, required   _____

15. waggish, facetious, droll, witty   _____

16. monetary, financial   _____

17. degeneration, deterioration; to wither   _____

18. to gripe, complain, kvetch, bellyache   _____

19. to aver, avow, affirm, avouch   _____

20. to peeve, vex, annoy, incense, gall, irk   _____

21. disorder, confusion, disorganization _____

22. caustic, acrimonious, acidulous, sardonic _____

Antonyms   *Choose the word for this unit that is most nearly*
__opposite__ in meaning to each of the following items.
Write it in the space given.

1. strife, discord, disagreement _____

2. calm, controlled; relaxed, leisurely _____

3. solemn, grave, earnest, humorless, grim _____

4. to please, delight; to soothe, pacify _____

5. erect, upright; energetic, dynamic _____

6. to deny, repudiate, disavow _____

7. to launch, kick off, initiate, begin _____

8. to liberate, release, free _____

9. repellent, repulsive, distasteful _____

10. growth, development; to mature, develop _____

11. order, organization, tidiness _____

12. optional; unnecessary _____

13. heartrending, poignant, pathetic _____

14. stouthearted, courageous, daring _____

15. bland, mild, gentle, soothing _____

Choosing the   *Encircle the __boldface__ word that more satisfactorily*
Right Word   *completes each of the following sentences.*

1. On the witness stand, the defendant (**asseverated, nettled**) his innocence so firmly and convincingly that it was difficult not to believe him.

2. We were able to (**consummate, glean**) only a few shreds of useful information from his long, pretentious speech.

3. During the 19th century, it was fashionable to spend a few weeks in the fall hunting (**grouse, nettles**), pheasants, and other game birds.

4. I noticed with approval that his (**pecuniary, mordant**) remarks were intended to deflate the pompous and unmask the hypocritical.

5. What we need to cope with this crisis is not cute (**grousing, stratagems**) but a bold, realistic plan and the courage to carry it out.

6. Of the 10 Congressional seats in our state, only one was won by a new member; all the other winners were (**incumbents, bastions**).

7. All that I needed to (**consummate, nettle**) the most important deal of my career was her signature on the dotted line.

8. The only way we'll really be able to increase productivity is to offer our employees a few solid (**frenetic, pecuniary**) incentives to work harder.

9. To feel fear in difficult situations is natural, but to allow one's conduct to be governed by fear is (**jocular, pusillanimous**).

10. In Victorian times, fashionable ladies (**disarrayed, incarcerated**) their waists in tight corsets to achieve a chic "hourglass" figure.

11. Comfortably (**recumbent, frenetic**) in the shade of the elm tree, I watched the members of the football team go through a hard, sweaty workout.

12. The affairs of our city are in such (**disarray, flotsam**) that the state may have to intervene to restore some semblance of order.

13. In the shelter, I saw for the first time people beaten and mutilated by life—the derelicts and (**flotsam, incumbents**) of the great city.

14. I have always regarded our schools and colleges as citadels of learning and (**bastions, stratagems**) against ignorance and superstition.

15. Before the ceremony began, we all bowed our heads and prayed for unity, peace, and (**concord, atrophy**) among all nations.

16. We were fascinated by the (**mordant, frenetic**) scene on the floor of the stock exchange as brokers struggled to keep up with sudden price changes.

17. There are few things in life as (**prepossessing, ludicrous**) as an unqualified person trying to assume the trappings of authority.

18. A born leader is someone who can rise to the (**incumbents, exigencies**) of any crisis that he or she may be confronted with.

19. The huge influx of wealth that resulted from foreign conquests led in part to the physical and moral (**atrophy, flotsam**) of the Roman ruling class.

20. Do you really think that those (**jocular, prepossessing**) remarks are appropriate on such a solemn occasion?

21. It has been said that the only way to handle a (**nettle, stratagem**), or any difficult problem, without being stung is to grasp it firmly and decisively.

22. Though Elizabeth I looked every inch the queen she in fact was, Victoria's appearance was not very (**recumbent, prepossessing**).

Unit 5

Definitions   *From the words in Group A and Group B following, choose the one that most nearly corresponds to each definition below. Write the word in the space at the right of the definition and in the illustrative phrase below it.*

Group A

acuity (ə 'kyü ə tē)
delineate (di 'lin ē āt)
depraved (di 'prāvd)
emend (ē 'mend)
enervate ('en ər vāt)
esoteric (es ə 'ter ik)

fecund ('fek ənd)
fiat ('fī at)
figment ('fig mənt)
garner ('gär nər)
hallow ('hal ō)

1. (v.) to portray, sketch, or describe in accurate and vivid detail; to represent pictorially

_____

_____ the main features of the plan

2. (v.) to set apart as holy or sacred, sanctify, consecrate; to honor greatly, revere

_____

_____ the field on which they fought

3. (v.) to correct; to alter to serve a new or different purpose

_____

_____ the report

4. (n.) a fabrication of the mind; an arbitrary notion

_____

just a(n) _____ of your imagination

5. (n.) an arbitrary order or decree; a command or act of will or consciousness

_____

the _____ of conscience

6. (adj.) intended for or understood by only a select few, private, secret

_____

_____ rites

7. (n.) sharpness (particularly of the mind or senses)

_____

the _____ of one's hearing

8. (v.) to acquire as the result of effort; to gather and store away, as for future use

_____

_____ wisdom

9. (adj.) fruitful in offspring or vegetation; intellectually productive

_____

a remarkably _____ brain

10. (v.) to weaken, lessen the mental, moral, or physical vigor of, enfeeble, hamstring

_____

a mind that has been _____ by disease

11. (*adj.*) brought to a state of evil and corruption, devoid
of moral principles

_____

led a(n) _____ life

Group B

idiosyncrasy (id ē ə 'siŋ krə sē)
ignominy ('ig nə min ē)
malediction (mal ə 'dik shən)
mundane (mən 'dān)
nuance ('nü äns)
overweening (ō vər 'wē niŋ)

penchant ('pen chənt)
reputed (ri 'pyüt id)
sophistry ('säf ə strē)
sumptuous ('səmp chü əs)
ubiquitous (yü 'bik wə təs)

12. (*adj.*) earthly, worldly, relating to practical and
material affairs; concerned with what is ordinary

_____

_____ concerns

13. (*n.*) a strong attraction or inclination

_____

a(n) _____ for belaboring the obvious

14. (*adj.*) present or existing everywhere

_____

the _____ eye of the TV camera

15. (*adj.*) according to reputation or general belief;
having widespread acceptance and good
reputation; (*part.*) alleged

_____

the _____ head of a crime syndicate

16. (*n.*) a curse, expression of hatred and condemnation

_____

hurl _____ at their enemies

17. (*adj.*) conceited, presumptuous; excessive,
immoderate

_____

_____ pride

18. (*n.*) reasoning that seems plausible but is actually
unsound; a fallacy

_____

beguiled by clever _____

19. (*n.*) a subtle or slight variation (as in color, meaning,
quality), delicate gradation or shade of difference

_____

a(n) _____ of meaning

20. (*adj.*) costly, rich, magnificent

_____

a(n) _____ feast

21. (*n.*) shame and disgrace

_____

the _____ resulting from the scandal

22. (*n.*) a peculiarity that serves to distinguish or identify

_____

the _____ of English grammar

Completing
the Sentence
Choose the word for this unit that best completes each
of the following sentences. Write it in the space given.

1. May I interrupt this abstruse discussion and turn your attention to more

_____ matters—like what's for dinner?

2. American-style fast-food shops have gained such popularity all over the

world that they are now truly _____ .

3. You have many good traits, but I do not admire your _____
for borrowing things and failing to return them.

4. His constant use of the word *fabulous*, even for quite ordinary subjects, is

a(n) _____ that I could do without.

5. The artist's sketch not only _____ the model's appearance
accurately but also captured something of her personality.

6. The passing years lessened her physical vigor but in no way diminished

the _____ of her judgment.

7. "Your suspicion that I am constantly making fun of you behind your back is

a mere _____ of your overheated brain," I replied.

8. I was so _____ by the oppressive heat and humidity of that
awful afternoon that I could barely move.

9. There is quite a difference between the austere furnishings of my little

apartment and the _____ accommodations of a luxury hotel.

10. Music can often express a(n) _____ of mood or feeling that
would be difficult to put into words.

11. He was a changed young man after he suffered the _____
of expulsion from West Point for conduct unbecoming a gentleman.

12. The ground in which those soldiers are buried was _____
by the blood they shed on it.

13. Most people I know are so busy dealing with the ordinary problems of life

that they have no time for _____ philosophical speculation.

14. Beneath the man's cultivated manner and impeccable grooming there

lurked the _____ mind of a brutal sadist.

15. Analysis will show that his "brilliant exposition" of how we can handle the

pollution problem without cost to anyone is the merest _____ .

16. Her report is in general accurate and well written, but there are several

respects in which I think it should be _____ .

17. The man is _____ to have mob connections, but so far no one has actually substantiated the allegation.

18. There he stood like some grim Old Testament prophet, impotently hurling _____ at the rival who had so cleverly outfoxed him.

19. During the eleven years of his "personal rule," King Charles I bypassed Parliament and ruled England by royal _____ .

20. The phonograph is but one of the wonderful new devices that sprang from the _____ mind of Thomas Edison, our most prolific inventor.

21. His _____ sense of superiority dominates his personality in much the same way as his beetling brow dominates his face.

22. The marathon not only brought in huge sums of money for Africa's starving masses but also _____ much sympathy for their plight.

Synonyms	*Choose the word from this unit that is most nearly **the same** in meaning as each of the following items. Write the word in the space provided.*

1. an eccentricity, quirk, mannerism   _____

2. ordinary, prosaic, humdrum, routine; earthly, sublunary   _____

3. an inclination, proclivity, propensity   _____

4. disgrace, dishonor, humiliation   _____

5. a command, decree, edict, ukase   _____

6. a fabrication, creation, invention   _____

7. lavish, munificent, opulent, splendid   _____

8. omnipresent, pervasive, universal   _____

9. a curse, imprecation, anathema   _____

10. corrupt, perverted, degenerated, vicious   _____

11. specious reasoning, casuistry   _____

12. sharpness, keenness, acuteness   _____

13. to consecrate, sanctify; to venerate   _____

14. unbridled, immoderate, inflated   _____

15. to correct, revise, rectify; to adapt   _____

16. occult; cryptic; arcane, recondite   _____

17. to impair; to hamstring, cripple, paralyze   _____

18. to collect, gather, accumulate

_____

19. a subtle variation, gradation, nicety

_____

20. to depict, portray, sketch, picture

_____

21. supposed, alleged, putative; reputable

_____

22. fruitful, fertile, teeming, prolific

_____

Antonyms *Choose the word for this unit that is most nearly **opposite** in meaning to each of the following items. Write it in the space given.*

1. moral, virtuous, upright; uncorrupted

_____

2. a blessing, benediction

_____

3. skimpy, meager, stingy, niggardly; spartan

_____

4. dullness, obtuseness

_____

5. barren, infertile, unproductive

_____

6. honor, glory, acclaim

_____

7. restricted, limited; rare, scarce

_____

8. proven, corroborated, authenticated

_____

9. to invigorate; to strengthen, buttress

_____

10. to spoil, mar, botch, mess up, damage

_____

11. to desecrate, defile, profane

_____

12. restrained, understated; modest, meek

_____

13. heavenly; unworldly, spiritual, transcendental

_____

14. accessible, comprehensible, intelligible

_____

15. to scatter, squander, waste, dissipate

_____

16. a natural disinclination

_____

Choosing the Right Word *Encircle the **boldface** word that more satisfactorily completes each of the following sentences.*

1. Your language is indeed clever and amusing, but your argument is nothing but a piece of outright (**sophistry, idiosyncrasy**).

2. In that rarefied atmosphere, I was afraid to ask about anything quite so (**sumptuous, mundane**) as the location of the john.

3. Probably no complaint of young people is more (**ubiquitous, depraved**) than "My parents don't understand me!"

4. Two synonyms are rarely exactly the same because (**fiats, nuances**) of tone or applicability make each of the words unique.

5. Few writers have J.D. Salinger's remarkable ability to (**delineate, emend**) the emotions and aspirations of the average teenager.

6. It is only in superior mental powers, not in physical strength or (**ignominy, acuity**) of the senses, that human beings surpass other living things.

7. In a democracy, the government must rule by persuasion and consent— not by mere (**fiat, sophistry**).

8. Someone with a pronounced (**penchant, figment**) for saying the wrong thing might justly be described as a victim of "foot-in-mouth" disease.

9. How I'd love to knock the wind out of the sails of that lout's (**fecund, overweening**) conceit!

10. Like a true fanatic, he considers anyone who disagrees with him on any issue to be either feebleminded or (**depraved, mundane**).

11. The conversation between the computer programmers was so (**esoteric, ubiquitous**) that I wasn't even sure whether they were speaking English.

12. We will never abandon a cause that has been (**garnered, hallowed**) by the achievements and sacrifices of so many noble people.

13. A true sign of intellectual maturity is the ability to distinguish the (**figments, maledictions**) of wishful thinking from reality.

14. Cleopatra took her own life rather than suffer the (**figment, ignominy**) of being led through the streets of Rome in chains.

15. Though Saint Paul borrowed that vivid image from Plato, he (**emended, garnered**) it to suit his own needs.

16. The alert defense put up by our team completely neutralized their opponents' (**reputedly, sumptuously**) unstoppable passing attack.

17. Her imagination is like a (**fecund, depraved**) field in which new ideas spring up like so many ripe ears of corn.

18. The tyrant noted wistfully that he was the object, not of his subjects' accolades, but of their (**maledictions, penchants**).

19. I appreciate all those kind expressions of gratitude for my services, but I had hoped also to (**emend, garner**) some greenbacks.

20. Scandal and corruption may so (**enervate, emend**) an administration that it can no longer function effectively.

21. He means well, but we cannot tolerate his highly (**idiosyncratic, fecund**) behavior in an organization that depends on discipline and teamwork.

22. The (**sumptuous, ubiquitous**) banquet was a pleasant change of pace from the spartan fare to which I had become accustomed.

Unit 6

Definitions   *From the words in Group A and Group B following, choose the one that most nearly corresponds to each definition below. Write the word on the line at the right of the definition and in the illustrative phrase below it.*

Group A

abject ('ab jekt)
agnostic (ag 'näs tik)
complicity (kəm 'plis ə tē)
derelict ('der ə likt)
diatribe ('dī ə trīb)
effigy ('ef ə jē)

equity ('ek wət ē)
inane (in 'ān)
indictment (in 'dīt mənt)
indubitable (in 'dü bə tə bəl)
intermittent (in tər 'mit ənt)

1. (*n.*) involvement in wrongdoing; the state of being an accomplice

accused of _____ in the crime

2. (*adj.*) silly, empty of meaning or value

a(n) _____ reply

3. (*n.*) one who believes that nothing is known about God; a skeptic; (*adj.*) without faith, skeptical

a confirmed _____

4. (*n.*) the act of accusing; a formal accusation

a(n) _____ for murder

5. (*n.*) the state or quality of being just, fair, or impartial; fair and equal treatment; something that is fair; the money value of a property above and beyond any mortgage or other claim

prompted by considerations of _____

6. (*adj.*) degraded, wretched; base, contemptible; cringing, servile; complete and unrelieved

living in _____ poverty

7. (*n.*) a bitter and prolonged verbal attack

a(n) _____ rather than an address

8. (*adj.*) stopping and beginning again, sporadic

_____ pains

9. (*n.*) someone or something that is abandoned or neglected; (*adj.*) left abandoned; neglectful of duty

a(n) _____ car

10. (*n.*) a crude image of a despised person

burn the enemy leader in _____

11. (*adj.*) certain, not to be doubted or denied

the _____ truth of the axiom

Group B

meretricious (mer ə 'trish əs)
moot (müt)
motif (mō 'tēf)
neophyte ('nē ə fīt)
perspicacity (pər spə 'kas ət ē)
plenary ('plēn ə rē)

prestigious (pre 'stij əs)
surveillance (sər 'vā ləns)
sylvan ('sil vən)
testy ('tes tē)
travesty ('trav ə stē)

12. (*n.*) a grotesque or grossly inferior imitation; a disguise, especially the clothing of the opposite sex; (*v.*) to ridicule by imitating in a broad or burlesque fashion

    make a(n) _____ of the ceremony

13. (*n.*) a watch kept over a person; careful, close, and disciplined observation

    kept under strict _____

14. (*adj.*) superficially attractive in a showy, cheap, or vulgar way; lacking sincerity; sham, spurious

    overly gaudy and _____ in style

15. (*n.*) a new convert, beginner, novice

    a mere _____ in comparison to me

16. (*adj.*) pertaining to or characteristic of forests; living or located in a forest; wooded, woody

    a(n) _____ path

17. (*adj.*) open to discussion and debate, unresolved; (*v.*) to bring up for discussion; (*n.*) a hypothetical law case argued by students

    a(n) _____ point

18. (*n.*) keenness in observing and understanding

    with all the _____ reputed to an owl

19. (*adj.*) easily irritated; characterized by impatience and exasperation

    a(n) _____ remark

20. (*adj.*) complete in all aspects or essentials; absolute; attended by all qualified members

    a(n) _____ session of the court

21. (*n.*) a principal idea or feature; a repeated or dominant figure in a design

    an Oriental _____ woven into the fabric

22. (*adj.*) having a highly favorable reputation, of high standing, commanding respect

    a(n) _____ book publisher

Completing the Sentence *Choose the word for this unit that best completes each of the following sentences. Write it in the space given.*

1. Since he neither affirms nor denies the existence of God, I'd classify him as a(n) _____ rather than an atheist.

2. It was such a(n) _____ remark that I couldn't keep myself from laughing derisively when I heard it.

3. How can you call that a(n) _____ question when it is quite clearly a simple matter of right and wrong?

4. Since the accused was never really given a chance to defend himself, his so-called "trial" was nothing but a(n) _____ of justice.

5. Those who saw the young woman being assaulted and did nothing to help her were in a sense guilty of _____ in the crime.

6. At the slightest sound of thunder, my dog Rover dives under the bed in a state of _____ terror.

7. Throughout the period that the terrorist thought he had gone undetected, he was actually under close _____ by the CIA.

8. Every time we did something to anger him, he delivered an intemperate _____ lambasting our "hopeless irresponsibility."

9. The fact that so many released prisoners return to a life of crime is in itself a terrifying _____ of our penal system.

10. I'd say that the phrase "having a short fuse" aptly describes my boss's decidedly _____ disposition.

11. During the emergency, the Mayor assumed _____ authority and did whatever was needed to provide essential services.

12. The novelty of the idea gave it a kind of _____ allure that belied its basic unsoundness.

13. "Simple _____ demands that we distribute the tax burden as fairly as possible among the populace," the Senator remarked.

14. I would be _____ in my duty to you if I did not warn you against the bad effects of smoking cigarettes.

15. The overthrown dictator was hanged in _____ before a vast throng in the town square.

16. In her garland of leaves and acorns, my little daughter looked very much like some _____ spirit out of our dim pagan past.

17. For years, we carried on a(n) _____ correspondence, sometimes allowing months to pass before a letter was answered.

18. In Wagner's operas, brief musical _____ associated with the characters or their actions recur again and again.

19. How could a mere _____ in the teaching profession
question the judgment of so experienced an educator?

20. Though many small liberal-arts colleges aren't as _____ as
Harvard or Yale, they are nonetheless first-rate educational institutions.

21. The _____ of her analysis not only clarified the nature of the
problem but also suggested its most promising solution.

22. Though some writers have emphasized Jefferson's human weaknesses, his
greatness is a(n) _____ part of the historic record.

Synonyms   *Choose the word for this unit that is most nearly **the
same** in meaning as each of the following items. Write it
in the space given.*

1. acuity, acumen, discernment   _____

2. wooded, forested, arcadian   _____

3. a theme, feature, element   _____

4. a burlesque, parody, caricature, farce   _____

5. a novice, tenderfoot, tyro, rookie   _____

6. irritable, peevish, waspish, petulant   _____

7. abandoned; remiss, delinquent; a bum   _____

8. involvement, connivance, collusion   _____

9. justice, fairness, impartiality   _____

10. debatable, questionable; to broach   _____

11. unlimited, unrestricted, absolute   _____

12. a figure, figurine, likeness, image   _____

13. idiotic, moronic, fatuous, vapid   _____

14. a skeptic or doubter about God   _____

15. fitful, spasmodic, sporadic, random   _____

16. monitoring, observation, scrutiny   _____

17. wretched, miserable; ignoble; sheer, utter   _____

18. a harangue, tirade   _____

19. a formal charge or accusation   _____

20. sham, spurious; tawdry, gaudy   _____

21. unquestionable, certain, indisputable _____

22. acclaimed, celebrated, much-touted _____

Antonyms   *Choose the word for this unit that is most nearly **opposite** in meaning to each of the following items. Write it in the space given.*

1. a panegyric, encomium, eulogy _____

2. sensible, meaningful; profound _____

3. continuous, uninterrupted _____

4. unknown, obscure _____

5. even-tempered, imperturbable, unexcitable _____

6. a veteran, pro, past master, expert _____

7. genuine, authentic, bona fide _____

8. injustice, unfairness; bias, prejudice _____

9. lofty, noble, exalted _____

10. someone who believes in the existence of God _____

11. lack of involvement or entanglement _____

12. undebatable, indisputable, self-evident _____

13. dullness, obtuseness _____

14. limited, restricted, incomplete _____

15. debatable, questionable, dubious _____

16. punctilious, conscientious, scrupulous _____

Choosing the Right Word   *Encircle the **boldface** word that more satisfactorily completes each of the following sentences.*

1. "I vetoed that idea when it was first (**mooted, indicted**) years ago," the Governor said, "and I have never regretted my decision."

2. Beneath his glib oratory and staggering erudition, I recognized the (**intermittent, meretricious**) appeal of the demagogue.

3. His extraordinary ability to (**moot, travesty**) the works of popular writers is largely due to his keen eye for the ridiculous.

4. Though the book was written by an avowed (**agnostic, derelict**), it enjoyed a certain popularity with the faithful.

5. Pathetic reminders of our dim nomadic past, bag ladies and other homeless (**motifs, derelicts**) roam our streets in increasing numbers.

6. Though I can sometimes be as (**testy, moot**) as an irate wasp, I normally do not lose my temper very easily.

7. His disgraceful behavior since he left college is in itself a(n) (**indictment, diatribe**) of the lax, overindulgent upbringing he received.

8. Since she is a fair-minded woman, I'm sure she will present both sides of the controversy with admirable (**equity, effigy**).

9. The historian had long been noted for the soundness of his scholarship and the (**complicity, perspicacity**) of his judgment.

10. Today's forecast calls for variable cloudiness with (**abject, intermittent**) periods of rain.

11. All of a sudden, a strange young man rushed onto the speaker's platform and launched into a(n) (**effigy, diatribe**) against "big government."

12. As he sat before the fire absent mindedly puffing on his pipe, Dad seemed the very epitome of (**plenary, sylvan**) contentment.

13. My studies have convinced me that the one dominant (**motif, diatribe**) in American history has been the expansion of democracy.

14. Only a(n) (**testy, abject**) coward would stand idly by as a defenseless old woman was mugged in the street.

15. After over 30 years in Congress, he retains the idealism of the (**agnostic, neophyte**) but has gained the practical wisdom of the veteran.

16. According to voodoo belief, one can get rid of an enemy by making a tiny (**effigy, motif**) of him and sticking it full of pins.

17. The picture shows the three Graces dancing in a forest clearing, while nymphs, satyrs, and other (**sylvan, testy**) creatures cavort among the trees.

18. The awkward pause in the conversation became even more painful when he interjected his (**moot, inane**) attempts at humor.

19. What qualities will he have to fall back on when his (**indubitable, testy**) charm and good looks begin to wear thin?

20. Instead of joining a (**meretricious, prestigious**) law firm, the young man took a job with an agency providing free legal services to the poor.

21. How can I be accused of (**indictment, complicity**) in that plot when I did not even know the conspirators?

22. Observers on the ground keep close (**surveillance, equity**) on air traffic at a busy airport by means of various electronic devices, such as radar.

Review Units 4–6

Analogies   *In each of the following, choose the item that best completes the comparison.*

1. agnostic is to **doubt** as
a. fundamentalist is to suspect
b. skeptic is to asseverate
c. convert is to ignore
d. atheist is to deny

2. nettle is to **irritation** as
a. appall is to delight
b. glean is to disapproval
c. intrigue is to fascination
d. nonplus is to boredom

3. sylvan is to **forest** as
a. nocturnal is to animal
b. urban is to city
c. rustic is to corrosion
d. maritime is to shore

4. sleeper is to **recumbent** as
a. typist is to sedentary
b. homebody is to nomadic
c. swimmer is to vertical
d. runner is to prone

5. pusillanimous is to **courage** as
a. fecund is to effectiveness
b. testy is to patience
c. ubiquitous is to occurrence
d. sumptuous is to appropriateness

6. travesty is to **ludicrous** as
a. nuance is to glaring
b. effigy is to stuffy
c. diatribe is to acerbic
d. penchant is to prepossessing

7. jocular is to **humor** as
a. mundane is to mystery
b. blithe is to sadness
c. esoteric is to contentment
d. pensive is to thought

8. malediction is to **curse** as
a. interdiction is to hallow
b. addiction is to emend
c. benediction is to bless
d. contradiction is to affirm

9. indubitable is to **moot** as
a. reputed is to alleged
b. ignominious is to disgraceful
c. esoteric is to mundane
d. prepossessing is to jocular

10. idiosyncrasy is to **eccentric** as
a. motif is to unusual
b. figment is to illusory
c. exigency is to optional
d. surveillance is to intermittent

11. acuity is to **perceive** as
a. perspicacity is to discern
b. complicity is to ignore
c. atrophy is to reinforce
d. equity is to observe

12. sadist is to **depraved** as
a. derelict is to prestigious
b. neophyte is to overweening
c. hero is to meretricious
d. coward is to pusillanimous

13. pecuniary is to **money** as
a. plenary is to astronomy
b. stationary is to finance
c. culinary is to cooking
d. ethical is to law

14. overweening is to **humility** as
a. frenetic is to composure
b. indubitable is to substance
c. prestigious is to honor
d. consummate is to skill

15. agnostic is to **faith** as
a. incumbent is to position
b. delineator is to ambition
c. sophist is to thought
d. neophyte is to experience

16. mordant is to **bite** as
a. inane is to scrape
b. trenchant is to cut
c. abject is to slice
d. fecund is to chop

17. mundane is to **earth** as
a. celestial is to sky
b. cosmic is to underworld
c. infernal is to universe
d. terrestrial is to sea

18. prison is to **incarcerate** as
a. hospital is to enervate
b. barn is to disarray
c. restaurant is to emend
d. silo is to garner

19. bastion is to **strong** as
a. indictment is to hurried
b. stratagem is to cunning
c. fiat is to cruel
d. effigy is to lively

20. grouse is to **discontent** as
a. crow is to pride
b. ape is to dislike
c. badger is to sorrow
d. parrot is to puzzlement

Identification   *In each of the following groups, encircle the word that is best defined or suggested by the introductory phrase.*

1. possesses a remarkable keenness of insight into human nature
a. concord   b. neophyte   c. diatribe   d. perspicacity

2. a question intended to cause embarrassment or annoyance
a. incarcerate   b. enervate   c. mundane   d. nettle

3. the sole defender of democracy in that part of the world
a. malediction   b. bastion   c. derelict   d. agnostic

4. wreckage that was washed up on the beach
a. adversity   b. nuance   c. disarray   d. flotsam

5. a cabin in a heavily forested or wooded area
a. mordant   b. overweening   c. abject   d. sylvan

6. a habit of stirring coffee with a fork, rather than a spoon
a. surveillance   b. complicity   c. atrophy   d. idiosyncrasy

7. a plan to keep our surprise party a secret
a. equity   b. stratagem   c. indictment   d. acuity

8. honored all over the country as the "dean" of Civil War historians
a. moot   b. prestigious   c. meretricious   d. intermittent

9. the need of the moment
a. exigency   b. ludicrous   c. prepossessing   d. reputed

10. a strong inclination toward the outdoor life
a. grouse   b. penchant   c. effigy   d. fiat

11. the woman who now represents this district in Congress
a. asseverate   b. pusillanimous   c. incumbent   d. garner

12. the product of a fevered brain or overactive imagination
a. travesty   b. flotsam   c. figment   d. ignominy

13. spent most of the summer lying on the beach
a. depraved   b. sumptuous   c. esoteric   d. recumbent

14. the literary theme of a man destroyed by his own ambitions
a. sophistry   b. motif   c. pecuniary   d. indubitable

15. never slowed down and relaxed
a. frenetic   b. consummate   c. plenary   d. jocular

16. keep a round-the-clock watch on the suspect
a. surveillance   b. diatribe   c. fiat   d. equity

17. a matter of dollars and cents
a. abject   b. intermittent   c. moot   d. pecuniary

Shades of Meaning   *Read each sentence carefully. Then encircle the item that best completes the statement below the sentence.*

Although the source was undeniably a reputed one, the managing editor declined to print the story without independent verification of its accuracy. **(2)**

1. The best definition for the word **reputed** in line 1 is
   a. alleged   b. supposed   c. reputable   d. anonymous

Many of this nation's Founding Fathers have been widely honored, but perhaps none has been so universally hallowed as its first president, George Washington. **(2)**

2. In line 2 the word **hallowed** most nearly means
   a. sanctified   b. emulated   c. consecrated   d. venerated

"I, King Pericles, have lost
This Queen, worth all our mundane cost."
        (Shakespeare, *Pericles,* III, 2, 70–71) **(2)**

3. The word **mundane** in line 2 most nearly means
   a. worldly   b. ordinary   c. routine   d. humdrum

The lender would agree to the loan only on the condition that the borrowers offer as security the equity they held in their home. **(2)**

4. In line 2 the word **equity** is used to mean
   a. impartiality   b. justice   c. furnishings   d. financial interest

The real business of the convention was conducted not so much in the plenary sessions as in preliminary, backroom caucuses. **(2)**

5. The word **plenary** in line 2 most nearly means
   a. absolute   b. unlimited   c. fully attended   d. unrestricted

---

Antonyms   *In each of the following groups, encircle the word or expression that is most nearly **opposite** in meaning to the **boldface word** in the introductory phrase.*

1. **consummate** a deal
   a. report   b. initiate   c. study   d. clinch

2. a **depraved** mind
   a. corrupt   b. intelligent   c. curious   d. virtuous

3. an **inane** remark
   a. explicit   b. unexpected   c. perceptive   d. fatuous

4. an **indubitable** argument
   a. doubtful   b. trenchant   c. surprising   d. new

5. the **acuity** of her mind
   a. orderliness   b. breadth   c. flexibility   d. obtuseness

6. **intermittent** rain
   a. sudden   b. continuous   c. seasonal   d. imminent

7. a **prepossessing** appearance
   a. repulsive   b. remarkable   c. timely   d. attractive

8. a **fecund** brain
a. fertile   b. large   c. barren   d. serious

9. a **prestigious** school
a. grand   b. obscure   c. modern   d. famous

10. a spirit of **concord**
a. strife   b. harmony   c. determination   d. curiosity

11. a **reputed** mobster
a. suspected   b. clever   c. powerful   d. proven

12. the **equity** of the decision
a. result   b. meaning   c. injustice   d. cause

13. a **ludicrous** scene
a. chaotic   b. heartrending   c. unusual   d. lengthy

14. mordant wit
a. bland   b. repellent   c. caustic   d. savage

15. the **ignominy** resulting from the deed
a. criticism   b. publicity   c. odium   d. acclaim

Completing the Sentence   *From the following words, choose the one that best completes each of the sentences below. Write the word in the space given.*

Group A

sophistry	malediction	pusillanimous	neophyte
meretricious	penchant	garner	idiosyncrasy

1. Do you remember the _____ lion in *The Wizard of Oz* whose ambition it was to become courageous?

2. At every graduation I have ever attended there seems to be one student who _____ more prizes than anyone else.

3. How can they tell us that such _____ represents careful scholarship and logical thinking?

4. Isn't it humiliating for you, as an experienced worker, to be outdone on the job by a mere _____ ?

5. English grammar has so many _____ that sometimes the exceptions to a general rule are as important as the rule itself.

Group B

flotsam	glean	delineate	overweening
jocular	motif	agnostic	travesty

1. His attempts at _____ remarks failed completely to relieve the prevailing gloom.

R

2. I will try to _____ a few items of information from your murkily written, poorly organized report.

3. Their imitation of democratic institutions is so feeble and insincere that it is no more than a(n) _____ of the real thing.

4. Let me try to _____ for you the main features of our plan for reorganizing the intramural sports program.

5. The various bits of _____ floating in the lake bear mute witness to the intensity of last night's storm.

Word Families

A. On the line provided, write a **noun form** of each of the following words.

EXAMPLE: consummate—**consummation**

1. fecund _____
2. depraved _____
3. testy _____
4. ubiquitous _____
5. reputed _____
6. mordant _____
7. jocular _____
8. delineate _____
9. emend _____
10. inane _____
11. asseverate _____
12. prestigious _____
13. incarcerate _____
14. sumptuous _____
15. enervate _____

B. On the line provided, write an **adjective** related to each of the following words.

EXAMPLE: equity—**equitable**

1. perspicacity _____
2. acuity _____
3. exigency _____
4. nettle _____
5. idiosyncrasy _____
6. ignominy _____

C. *On the line provided, write a **verb** related to each of the following words.*

Example: malediction—**maledict**

1. indictment _____

2. prepossessing _____

3. depraved _____

4. reputed _____

5. intermittent _____

6. indubitable _____

Filling the Blanks   *Encircle the pair of words that best complete each of the following passages.*

1. Although the man is certainly thought to have been involved in the crime, no _____ has yet been brought against him because the authorities have not been able to assemble enough evidence to establish his _____ beyond a reasonable doubt.

    a. indictment . . . complicity   c. malediction . . . acuity
    b. surveillance . . . equity   d. figment . . . perspicacity

2. Despite the harried officer's _____ attempts to steady his troops after the left flank had been turned, they fled from the field in such _____ that their departure was more of a rout than a retreat.

    a. consummate . . . ignominy   c. intermittent . . . concord
    b. ludicrous . . . equity   d. frenetic . . . disarray

3. After the battle, the officer who had failed to carry out his orders was arrested by the military police, charged with _____ of duty, and _____ in the stockade, pending a court martial.

    a. atrophy . . . garnered   c. travesty . . . mooted
    b. dereliction . . . incarcerated   d. malediction . . . hallowed

4. Vincent van Gogh was indeed a(n) _____ technician, able to _____ every nuance of nature's variegated panorama with a mere stroke of the brush.

    a. meretricious . . . emend   c. consummate . . . delineate
    b. indubitable . . . enervate   d. prestigious . . . travesty

5. I'm extremely circumspect about what I say or do in the office because my boss is so _____ that it is easy to _____ or exasperate him.

    a. mordant . . . emend   c. testy . . . nettle
    b. abject . . . moot   d. jocular . . . enervate

Analogies   *In each of the following, choose the item that best completes the comparison.*

1. consummate is to **perfection** as
a. myopic is to perspicacity
b. esoteric is to accessibility
c. plenary is to completeness
d. taciturn is to propriety

2. germane is to **relevance** as
a. coherent is to consistency
b. meretricious is to genuineness
c. piquant is to humanity
d. utopian is to practicality

3. pejorative is to **derogatory** as
a. jocular is to ludicrous
b. moot is to indubitable
c. abject is to lofty
d. pusillanimous is to craven

4. inane is to **acuity** as
a. overt is to brevity
b. prestigious is to status
c. banal is to originality
d. prepossessing is to allure

5. articulate is to **mouth** as
a. taste is to lip
b. scan is to eye
c. grouse is to heel
d. accost is to foot

6. detective is to **surveillance** as
a. saint is to sacrilege
b. scout is to reconnaissance
c. witch is to covenant
d. artist is to travesty

7. testy is to **nettle** as
a. serene is to disturb
b. callous is to move
c. articulate is to numb
d. sensitive is to hurt

8. acquisitive is to **garner** as
a. perspicacious is to glean
b. agnostic is to dissemble
c. depraved is to emend
d. distraught is to cavort

9. intransigent is to **compromise** as
a. insatiable is to carp
b. intractable is to cooperate
c. incumbent is to oblige
d. irresolute is to temporize

10. diatribe is to **animadversions** as
a. eulogy is to rebukes
b. harangue is to accolades
c. encomium is to compliments
d. panegyric is to reprimands

Shades of Meaning   *Read each sentence carefully. Then encircle the item that best completes the statement below the sentence.*

In the comedies—especially those that involve mistaken identity—Shakespeare often hinges a turn of plot on the appearance of a character in travesty. **(2)**

1. In line 3 the word **travesty** is used to mean
a. burlesque   b. disguise   c. farce   d. caricature

George Eliot introduces the hero of her 1861 novel *Silas Marner* as a miserly, avid weaver who cares for nothing on earth so much as his hoard of gold coin. **(2)**

2. The word **avid** in line 2 is best defined as
a. enthusiastic   b. keen   c. eager   d. grasping

The Transcontinental Treaty of 1819, a territorial concord between Spain and America that for the first time drew the boundary of the United States from ocean to ocean, was chiefly the work of future President John Quincy Adams. **(2)**

3. The word **concord** in line 1 is used to mean
a. harmony   b. unanimity   c. pact   d. misunderstanding

"What judgement shall I dread, doing no wrong?
You have among you many a purchased slave,   (2)
Which, like your asses and your dogs and mules,
You use in abject and in slavish parts   (4)
Because you bought them. . . . "
    (Shakespeare, *The Merchant of Venice*, IV, 1, 89–93)

4. In line 4 the word **abject** most nearly means
    a. servile   b. unrelieved   c. wretched   d. cringing

The chief incumbency of the President is, in the succinct words of the
inaugural oath, "to preserve, protect, and defend the Constitution of the   (2)
United States."

5. The best definition for the word **incumbency** in line 1 is
    a. term   b. officeholder   c. aide   d. duty

**Filling
the Blanks**
*Encircle the pair of words that best complete each of
the following passages.*

1. It is a truly sad commentary on modern city life that bag ladies and other
homeless _____ are becoming as _____ as
traffic lights on the streets of our larger urban centers.
    a. suppliants . . . histrionic   c. derelicts . . . ubiquitous
    b. agnostics . . . prestigious   d. incumbents . . . overweening

2. Even after the last _____ of enemy resistance had fallen to
our troops, the sound of _____ sniper fire occasionally
broke the stillness of the summer evening.
    a. bastion . . . intermittent   c. maelstrom . . . incendiary
    b. gambit . . . meretricious   d. nuance . . . recumbent

3. So much industrial waste has been dumped into that once clear lake that it
has now become a _____ cesspool covered with all kinds
of unsightly and potentially dangerous _____ .
    a. primordial . . . concord   c. fecund . . . verbiage
    b. verdant . . . largesse   d. murky . . . flotsam

4. Though most Northerners were not _____ proponents of war
with the South, many of them responded to President Lincoln's call to arms
with exemplary _____ .
    a. mordant . . . ignominy   c. prepossessing . . . exigency
    b. avid . . . celerity   d. reputed . . . disarray

5. Since the Roman emperors were autocrats who ruled their vast empire by
_____ , the democratic institutions of the Republic slowly
_____ and died.
    a. complicity . . . dissembled   c. fiat . . . atrophied
    b. penchant . . . evinced   d. sophistry . . . groused

Unit 7

Definitions *From the words in Group A and Group B following, choose the one that most nearly corresponds to each definition below. Write the word in the space at the right of the definition and in the illustrative phrase below it.*

Group A

allay (ə 'lā)
bestial ('bes chəl)
convivial (kən 'viv ē əl)
coterie ('kō tə rē)
counterpart ('kaunt ər pärt)
demur (di 'mər)

effrontery (ə 'frən tə rē)
embellish (em 'bel ish)
ephemeral (i 'fem ər əl)
felicitous (fə 'lis ə təs)
furtive ('fər tiv)

1. (*n.*) a person or thing closely resembling or corresponding to another; a complement _____

my _____ on the other team

2. (*n.*) shameless boldness, impudence _____

have the _____ to talk back

3. (*adj.*) lasting only a short time, short-lived _____

achieved only a(n) _____ popularity

4. (*adj.*) appropriate, apt, well chosen; marked by well-being or good fortune, happy _____

a(n) _____ turn of events

5. (*v.*) to calm or pacify, set to rest; to lessen or relieve _____

_____ one's hunger

6. (*adj.*) done slyly or stealthily, sneaky, secret, shifty; stolen _____

a(n) _____ glance

7. (*n.*) a circle of acquaintances; a close-knit, often exclusive, group of people with a common interest _____

Robert Browning and his _____

8. (*v.*) to decorate, adorn, touch up; to improve by adding details _____

_____ a story

9. (*v.*) to object or take exception to; (*n.*) an objection _____

_____ at the decision

10. (*adj.*) festive, sociable, having fun together, genial _____

a(n) _____ gathering

11. (*adj.*) beastlike; beastly, brutal; subhuman in intelligence and sensibility _____

a(n) _____ act

58

Group B

garish ('gar ish)
illusory (i 'lü sə rē)
indigent ('in də jənt)
inordinate (in 'ôr də nət)
jettison ('jet ə sən)
misanthrope ('mis ən thrōp)

pertinacious (pər tə 'nā shəs)
picayune (pik ē 'yün)
raiment ('rā mənt)
threshold ('thresh hōld)
wraith (rāth)

12. (*n.*) clothing, garments   _____

tore their _____ in anguish

13. (*adj.*) glaring; tastelessly showy or overdecorated in a vulgar or offensive way   _____

_____ colors

14. (*adj.*) needy, impoverished   _____

the homeless and the _____

15. (*n.*) a person who hates or despises people   _____

a(n) _____ like Timon of Athens

16. (*adj.*) of little value or importance, paltry, measly; concerned with trifling matters, small-minded   _____

a(n) _____ fault

17. (*adj.*) very persistent; holding firmly to a course of action or a set of beliefs; hard to get rid of, refusing to be put off or denied   _____

as _____ as a bulldog

18. (*n.*) a ghostly apparition, specter   _____

as pale as a(n) _____

19. (*adj.*) far too great, exceeding reasonable limits, excessive   _____

_____ praise

20. (*n.*) the board or stone that lies under a door, sill; the place or point of entering or beginning, outset; the point at which a physiological or psychological effect is produced, brink   _____

at the very _____ of consciousness

21. (*adj.*) misleading, deceptive; lacking or not based on reality   _____

a(n) _____ sense of security

22. (*v.*) to cast overboard, get rid of as unnecessary or burdensome   _____

_____ the ballast

**Completing
the Sentence**

*Choose the word for this unit that best completes each
of the following sentences. Write it in the space given.*

1. At the Casablanca Conference in 1943 President Roosevelt and his
   military aides met with their British _____ to map military
   strategy for the Western Allies.

2. Jonathan Swift so came to loathe human folly, vice, and hypocrisy that he
   died a virtual _____ .

3. "If at first you don't succeed, try, try again" seems to be the motto of that
   _____ young woman.

4. The _____ manner in which he sidled into the room and
   tried to avoid being noticed actually drew attention to his presence.

5. In the Victorian era, designers _____ women's dresses with
   all sorts of elaborate frills and flounces.

6. Recent developments in that part of the world have intensified rather than
   _____ our fears of a renewed conflict.

7. A busy executive in today's high-pressure business world just doesn't have
   time to deal with such _____ concerns as making coffee.

8. The _____ movie palaces of an earlier era have given way
   to smaller theaters, decorated in a simpler, more austere style.

9. Many a now-forgotten "movie great" has discovered to his or her chagrin
   that fame may indeed be as _____ as a passing shower.

10. He had the _____ to come into my own home to tell me
    what I should do to help him.

11. When Charles V retired to a Spanish monastery, he exchanged the costly
    _____ of a king for the simple habit of a monk.

12. To bring luck to a marriage, it is customary for a groom to carry his new
    bride across the _____ of their first home together.

13. The "Old 400" was a very small and exclusive _____ of
    prominent families that dominated East Coast society for decades.

14. He is entitled to reasonable compensation for the damage to his car, but
    the demands he has made are totally _____ .

15. Though I don't consider myself much of a diplomat, I think I handled that
    delicate situation in a particularly _____ manner.

16. The disastrous stock market crash of 1929 left many a wealthy speculator
    as _____ as the proverbial church mouse.

17. Since we all agreed that the proposal seemed to offer the best solution to
    our problem, it was accepted without _____ .

18. The man's features suddenly contorted into a(n) _____ leer, more reminiscent of a hobgoblin than a human being.

19. The thin columns of smoke hovering over the chimneys on that black night resembled pale _____ come from beyond the grave.

20. The crew of the sinking freighter _____ most of the cargo in a desperate effort to keep the sinking ship afloat.

21. A good deal of sad experience has taught me that my youthful hopes of getting something for nothing are entirely _____ .

22. Who wouldn't have had fun among such a(n) _____ group of people?

Synonyms   *Choose the word from this unit that is most nearly **the same** in meaning as each of the following items. Write it in the space given.*

1. penniless, poverty-stricken, destitute _____

2. fanciful, imaginary, specious, spurious _____

3. persistent, stubborn, dogged, determined _____

4. paltry, inconsequential, piddling, trifling _____

5. a person who despises people _____

6. to adorn, ornament, decorate, garnish _____

7. fleeting, transient, evanescent, transitory _____

8. to protest, object to _____

9. a doorsill; the outset, commencement _____

10. fortunate, happy; apposite, well-put _____

11. apparel, attire, clothing, garments _____

12. excessive, exorbitant, extravagant _____

13. beastlike, animal; depraved, loathsome _____

14. a clique, set, circle _____

15. gaudy, flashy, tawdry; glaring _____

16. sneaky, clandestine, covert, surreptitious _____

17. a person's "opposite number" _____

18. gall, chutzpah, nerve, impertinence, cheek _____

19. to lessen, reduce, alleviate, moderate _____

20. funloving, jovial, genial, merry _____

21. to cast off, discard, dump, junk, abandon _____

22. a phantom, specter, ghost _____

Antonyms *Choose the word from this unit that is most nearly* **opposite** *in meaning to each of the following items. Write it in the space given.*

1. shyness, diffidence, timidity _____

2. subdued, muted, understated, quiet _____

3. to assent to, consent to, accept, agree to _____

4. durable, long-lasting, permanent, perpetual _____

5. moderate, reasonable, equitable _____

6. to undecorate, strip; to mar, disfigure _____

7. human; humane, clement; virtuous, upright _____

8. too willing to throw in the towel _____

9. dour, grim, sullen, unsociable _____

10. inept, inappropriate, graceless; unhappy _____

11. forthright, aboveboard, open _____

12. wealthy, affluent, prosperous _____

13. important, significant; huge, gigantic _____

14. actual, real, factual, objective _____

15. to aggravate, exacerbate, intensify _____

16. to conserve, retain, hold on to, keep _____

Choosing the Right Word *Encircle the* **boldface** *word that more satisfactorily completes each of the following sentences.*

1. The Presidency is the "toughest job in the world" because it makes such (**garish, inordinate**) demands on a person's time, energy, and ingenuity.

2. With the emergence of computer technology in the 1980's, the world arrived at the (**wraith, threshold**) of a new era in the history of communication.

3. An emotion so fickle and (**ephemeral, pertinacious**) does not deserve to be dignified by the name of "love."

4. "You mean you had the (**effrontery, demur**) to ask for a raise when everyone knows you've been goofing off lately?" I asked in amazement.

5. The kind of (**garish, felicitous**) theatrical makeup used by circus clowns is not suitable for an elegant fashion model.

6. The proofreader didn't notice any significant flaws in the writing, but he did find a few (**ephemeral, picayune**) defects in the typesetting.

7. Nothing we could say seemed to (**demur, allay**) her grief over the loss of her pet dog.

8. To anyone as fond of horses as I am, the stable and the tack room provide as (**indigent, convivial**) an atmosphere as one could wish for.

9. If installment buying is not carefully controlled, the benefits that can accrue from it may prove wholly (**illusory, inordinate**).

10. I am flattered that you want me to chair the meeting, but I must (**demur, embellish**) on the grounds of my youth and inexperience.

11. When the facts of a matter speak so plainly for themselves, we shouldn't seek to (**allay, embellish**) them.

12. I can always come up with the crushing rejoinder, the dazzling witticism, or the (**furtive, felicitous**) phrase—about an hour after I need it!

13. Somehow, it depresses me to think that with the approach of winter this magnificent old tree will surrender all its leafy (**effrontery, raiment**).

14. She has neither the starry-eyed optimism of the idealist nor the mordant cynicism of the (**wraith, misanthrope**).

15. Though the Federal government does much to help the (**indigent, illusory**), private charities play no small part in seeing to their welfare.

16. At that point in our relations, the first tentative misgivings—the merest (**wraith, coterie**) of a suspicion—began to enter my mind.

17. Every dynamic and successful society must be able to (**jettison, allay**) ideas and institutions that have outlived their usefulness.

18. As the rock star's popularity began to skyrocket, what had been a small (**coterie, raiment**) of admirers became an unruly mob.

19. The atrocities committed by the (**garish, bestial**) commandants of such concentration camps as Auschwitz appalled the civilized world.

20. When I returned to the office earlier than expected, I caught the little snoop (**felicitously, furtively**) going through the papers on my desk.

21. The famous sleuth pursued his investigation with all the (**pertinacity, conviviality**) of a lion stalking its dinner.

22. Often the antonym of a given English word is not so much its opposite as its (**embellishment, counterpart**)—for example, *actor* and *actress*.

Unit 8

Definitions *From the words in Group A and Group B following, choose the one that most nearly corresponds to each definition below. Write the word in the space at the right of the definition and in the illustrative phrase below it.*

Group A

allege (ə 'lej)
arrant ('ar ənt)
badinage (bad ə 'näzh)
conciliate (kən 'sil ē āt)
countermand ('kaün tər mand)
echelon ('esh ə län)

exacerbate (eg 'zas ər bāt)
fatuous ('fach ü əs)
irrefutable (ir i 'fyü tə bəl)
juggernaut ('jəg ər nôt)
lackadaisical (lak ə 'dā zə kəl)

1. (*n.*) one of a series of levels or grades in an organization or field of activity; an organized military unit; a steplike formation or arrangement _____

   the lower _____ of government

2. (*adj.*) that cannot be disproved; beyond argument _____

   a(n) _____ alibi

3. (*n.*) light and playful conversation _____

   dialogue full of delightful _____

4. (*v.*) to assert without proof or confirmation _____

   _____ a mob connection

5. (*adj.*) stupid or foolish in a self-satisfied way _____

   a(n) _____ remark

6. (*adj.*) lacking spirit or interest, halfhearted _____

   a(n) _____ performance

7. (*n.*) a massive and inescapable force or object that crushes whatever is in its path _____

   the _____ of war

8. (*v.*) to make more violent, severe, bitter, or painful _____

   _____ a quarrel

9. (*v.*) to overcome the distrust of, win over; to appease, pacify; to reconcile, make consistent _____

   try to _____ an enemy

10. (*adj.*) thoroughgoing, out-and-out; shameless, blatant _____

    a(n) _____ scoundrel

11. (*v.*) to cancel or reverse one order or command with another that is contrary to the first _____

    _____ my previous instructions

Group B

litany ('lit ə nē)
macabre (mə 'käb rə)
melange (mā 'länzh)
paucity ('pô sə tē)
portend (pôr 'tend)
raze (rāz)

recant (ri 'kant)
saturate ('sach ə rāt)
saturnine ('sat ər nīn)
slough (sləf)
substantive ('səb stən tiv)

12. (adj.) of gloomy or surly disposition; cold or sluggish in mood _____

of a decidedly _____ temperament

13. (n.) a prayer consisting of short appeals to God recited by the leader alternating with responses from the congregation; any repetitive chant; a long list _____

recite an interminable _____ of grievances

14. (adj.) grisly, gruesome; horrible, distressing; having death as a subject _____

a(n) _____ story

15. (adj.) pertaining to the essence or substance of something; existing in its own right; real, not apparent; solid; of major importance _____

_____ evidence

16. (v.) to withdraw a statement or belief to which one has previously been committed, renounce, retract _____

_____ one's previous assertions

17. (n.) an inadequate quantity, scarcity, dearth _____

a(n) _____ of ideas

18. (v.) to tear down, destroy completely; to cut or scrape off or out _____

_____ the old schoolhouse

19. (v.) to indicate beforehand that something is about to happen; to give advance warning of _____

_____ disaster

20. (n.) a mixture, medley _____

a strange _____ of fact and fiction

21. (v.) to soak thoroughly, fill to capacity; to satisfy fully _____

a sponge that is _____ with water

22. (v.) to cast off, discard; to get rid of something objectionable or unnecessary; to plod through or as if through mud; (n.) a mire; a state of depression _____

_____ off old habits

8

Completing the Sentence   *Choose the word for this unit that best completes each of the following sentences. Write it in the space given.*

1. Ms. Ryan's warnings to the class to "review thoroughly" seemed to me to

_____ an unusually difficult examination.

2. At first I thought it would be easy to shoot holes in their case, but I soon

realized that their arguments were just about _____ .

3. The service in honor of the miners trapped in the underground collapse

included prayers and _____ imploring divine mercy.

4. The meal consisted of a(n) _____ of dishes, each of which was typical of a different ethnic group living in the area.

5. Her friendly manner and disarming smile helped to _____ those who opposed her views on the proposal.

6. As a snake _____ off its old skin, so Tony hoped to rid himself of his weaknesses and develop a new and better personality.

7. The seriousness of the matter under discussion left no room for the type of

lighthearted _____ encountered in the locker room.

8. "I wish this were merely a matter of fixing a few details," I said, "but,

unfortunately, we must make _____ changes in the text."

9. You are not going to do well in your job if you continue to work in such

a(n) _____ and desultory manner.

10. However much it may cost me, I will never _____ the principles to which I have devoted my life.

11. No sooner had the feckless tsar decreed a general mobilization than he

_____ his order, only to reissue it a short time later.

12. Only someone with a truly _____ sense of humor would decide to use a hearse as the family car or a coffin as a bed.

13. "It seems to me that such _____ hypocrisy is indicative of a thoroughly opportunistic approach to running for office," I said sadly.

14. Though some "home remedies" appear to alleviate the symptoms of a

disease, they may in fact _____ the condition.

15. The men now being held in police custody are _____ to have robbed eight supermarkets over the last year.

16. The air show featured some spectacular aerial acrobatics, including such

old favorites as barnstorming and turning in _____ .

17. His four disastrous years in office were marked by a plenitude of promises

and a(n) _____ of performance.

18. We object to the policy of _____ historic old buildings to make way for unsightly parking lots.

19. The enemy's lines crumpled up before the mighty _____ of our attack like so much wheat before a harvester.

20. My shirt became so _____ with perspiration on that beastly day that I had to change it more than once during the match.

21. After he made that absurd remark, a(n) _____ grin of self-congratulation spread like syrup across the lumpy pancake of his face.

22. "I find it terribly depressing to be around people whose dispositions are so _____ and misanthropic," I remarked.

Synonyms   *Choose the word for this unit that is most nearly the* ***same*** *in meaning as each of the following items. Write it in the space given.*

1. indisputable, incontrovertible, undeniable   _____

2. to retract, withdraw, repudiate, disavow   _____

3. sullen, morose, surly, gloomy   _____

4. listless, indolent, indifferent, lax   _____

5. a scarcity, lack, dearth   _____

6. a level of command; a steplike formation   _____

7. banter, persiflage, repartee   _____

8. to pull down, demolish; to shave off   _____

9. a destructive force that is unavoidable   _____

10. to aggravate, intensify, worsen   _____

11. to reverse, recall, revoke   _____

12. a medley, farrago, potpourri, hodgepodge   _____

13. out-and-out, thoroughgoing, egregious   _____

14. solid, firm, substantial; real; major   _____

15. grotesque, grim, grisly, ghoulish   _____

16. a rigmarole, catalog, megillah   _____

17. silly, vapid, inane, doltish, stupid, vacuous   _____

18. to assert, claim, contend   _____

19. to bode, foretell, foreshadow, suggest   _____

20. to placate, pacify, appease; to reconcile   _____

21. to permeate, drench, flood, imbue _____

22. to shed, cast off, discard; to slog _____

Antonyms   *Choose the word from this unit that is most nearly* **opposite** *in meaning to each of the following items. Write it in the space given.*

1. energetic, vigorous; wholehearted _____

2. an abundance, glut, plenitude, deluge _____

3. lighthearted, cheerful, vivacious _____

4. to build, construct, raise, erect _____

5. indefensible, untenable; disputable _____

6. to antagonize, alienate, estrange _____

7. to reaffirm, reassert _____

8. sensible, intelligent, perceptive, bright _____

9. flimsy, insubstantial; minor _____

10. to alleviate, mitigate, ameliorate _____

11. a serious conversation; a sermon _____

12. to prove beyond the shadow of a doubt; to deny _____

13. to take on, acquire, assume _____

14. to spread thinly over; to drain _____

Choosing the Right Word   *Encircle the* **boldface** *word that more satisfactorily completes each of the following sentences.*

1. Their so-called philosophy of life is no more than a (**melange, paucity**) of half-baked and incongruous ideas drawn from the most disparate sources.

2. The authority of the Student Council is not absolute because the principal can (**countermand, exacerbate**) any of its decisions.

3. His debating technique is based on the firm belief that anything bellowed in a loud voice is absolutely (**saturnine, irrefutable**).

4. The views of the two parties involved in this dispute are so diametrically opposed that it will be almost impossible to (**conciliate, saturate**) them.

5. His attempts at casual (**badinage, echelon**) did not conceal the fact that he was acutely embarrassed by his blunder.

6. We have many capable and well-meaning people in our organization, but it seems to me that there is a (**paucity, litany**) of real leadership.

7. Economists believe that the drop in automobile sales and steel production (**countermands, portends**) serious problems for business in the future.

8. Not surprisingly, the committee's final report was an incongruous mixture of the astute and the (**irrefutable, fatuous**).

9. With incredible unconcern, the nobles of Europe immersed themselves in social frivolities as the fearful (**juggernaut, litany**) of World War I steam-rolled ineluctably toward them.

10. Over the years, hard work and unstinting devotion to duty have raised me from one (**echelon, melange**) of company management to the next.

11. By (**portending, sloughing**) off the artificiality of her first book, the novelist arrived at a style that was simple, genuine, and highly effective.

12. By denying your guilt without offering any explanation of your actions, you will only (**recant, exacerbate**) an already bad situation.

13. The continuing popularity of horror movies suggests that one way to score at the box office is to exploit the (**macabre, lackadaisical**).

14. It is a good deal easier to (**raze, allege**) an old building than it is to destroy a time-honored social institution.

15. Someone with such a (**substantive, saturnine**) outlook on life doesn't make an agreeable traveling companion, especially on a long journey.

16. Only a(n) (**arrant, lackadaisical**) knave would be capable of devising such an incredibly underhanded and treacherous scheme.

17. In earlier times, people whose views conflicted with "received opinion" often had to (**recant, portend**) their ideas or face the consequences.

18. Our excitement at visiting the world-famous ruins was dampened by the (**lackadaisical, arrant**) attitude of the bored and listless guide.

19. What possible purpose will be served by setting up yet another hamburger stand in an area already (**saturated, alleged**) with fast-food shops?

20. She excused herself from lending me the money I so desperately needed by (**portending, alleging**) that she had financial troubles of her own.

21. I never ask anyone "How are you?" anymore because I am afraid I will be treated to an endless (**litany, paucity**) of symptoms and ailments.

22. Though he threw around a lot of facts and figures, they really contributed nothing (**fatuous, substantive**) to the discussion.

Unit 9

Definitions   *From the words in Group A and Group B following, choose the one that most nearly corresponds to each definition below. Write the word in the space at the right of the definition and in the illustrative phrase below it.*

Group A

acclamation (ak lə 'mā shən)
bucolic (byü 'käl ik)
calumniate (kə 'ləm nē āt)
chary ('châr ē)
collusion (kə 'lü zhən)
dilettante ('dil ə tänt)

imperturbable (im pər 'tər bə bəl)
increment ('in krə mənt)
mandate ('man dāt)
paltry ('pôl trē)
paroxysm ('par ək siz əm)

1. (*adj.*) not easily excited; emotionally steady

_____

remained _____ throughout

2. (*n.*) a sudden outburst; a spasm, convulsion

_____

a(n) _____ of laughter

3. (*n.*) an enlargement, increase, addition

_____

in _____ of five

4. (*n.*) secret agreement or cooperation

_____

_____ with the enemy

5. (*n.*) a dabbler in the arts; one who engages in an activity in an amateurish, trifling way

_____

a mere _____

6. (*n.*) a shout of welcome; an overwhelming verbal vote of approval

_____

elected by _____

7. (*adj.*) characteristic of the countryside, rural, rustic; relating to shepherds and cowherds, pastoral

_____

the Greek _____ poets

8. (*adj.*) trifling, insignificant; mean, despicable; inferior, trashy

_____

a(n) _____ sum of money

9. (*v.*) to slander; to accuse falsely and maliciously

_____

seek to _____ a person's memory

10. (*n.*) an authoritative command, formal order, authorization; (*v.*) to issue such an order

_____

under a UN _____

11. (*adj.*) extremely cautious, hesitant, or slow with; reserved, diffident

_____

_____ of the proposal

Group B

pedantry ('ped ən trē)
peregrination (per ə grə 'nā shən)
profane (prō 'fān)
proffer ('präf ər)
redolent ('red ə lənt)
refulgent (ri 'fəl jənt)

shibboleth ('shib ə leth)
tyro ('tī rō)
unremitting (ən ri 'mit iŋ)
vacillate ('vas ə lāt)
vituperative (vī 'tü pər ə tiv)

12. (*n.*) a word, expression, or custom that distinguishes a particular group of persons from all others; a commonplace saying, truism _____

campaign slogans and other _____

13. (*adj.*) shining, radiant, resplendent _____

_____ in the morning light

14. (*n.*) a beginner, novice; one with little or no background or skill _____

a(n) _____ at the game

15. (*n.*) the act of traveling; an excursion, especially on foot or to a foreign country _____

my recent _____ in the Near East

16. (*adj.*) fragrant, smelling strongly; tending to arouse memories or create an aura _____

_____ of lilacs

17. (*v.*) to present or offer _____

_____ advice

18. (*n.*) a pretentious display of knowledge; overly rigid attention to rules and details _____

_____ rather than true scholarship

19. (*adj.*) impure, defiled; worldly, not connected with religious or spiritual matters; (*v.*) to treat with irreverence or contempt _____

_____ a holy place

20. (*adj.*) not stopping, maintained steadily, never letting up, relentless _____

pain that is _____

21. (*adj.*) harshly abusive, severely scolding _____

an angry and _____ speech

22. (*v.*) to swing indecisively from one idea or course of action to another; to waver weakly in mind or will _____

tends to _____ in a crisis

Completing the Sentence *Choose the word for this unit that best completes each of the following sentences. Write it in the space given.*

1. The contractor was suspected of having acted in _____ with a state official to fix the bids on certain public works contracts.

2. Even the merest _____ in the use of firearms knows that a gun should never be pointed at another person.

3. As we waited through the long night for the arrival of the rescue party, we _____ between hope and despair.

4. As a(n) _____ summer sun sank slowly in the west, the skies were ablaze with color.

5. The Pledge of Allegiance is no mere _____ to be recited mechanically and without understanding like some advertising jingle.

6. Seized by a(n) _____ of rage, he began to beat the bars of his cell with his bare hands.

7. The scene may seem ordinary to you, but I find it _____ with memories of happy summers spent in these woods.

8. Since Lucy had expected no more than polite applause, she was delighted by the _____ she received from the audience.

9. I have learned from long experience to be extremely _____ about offering advice when it has not been requested.

10. I think language that might be acceptable in ordinary circumstances is disrespectful, even _____ , in such hallowed surroundings.

11. It is sheer _____ to insist upon applying the rules of formal literary composition to everyday speech and writing.

12. The painting shows a restfully _____ scene, with some cows grazing placidly in a meadow as their herder dozes under a bush.

13. She may have great musical talents, but she will get nowhere so long as she has the casual attitude of the _____ .

14. Every time I sign a new lease on my apartment, my rent goes up, though the _____ are not usually very large.

15. However long and hard the struggle, we must be _____ in our efforts to wipe out racism in this country.

16. Since Lincoln is now considered a great national hero, it is hard to believe that he was bitterly _____ when he was President.

17. "The overwhelming victory I have won at the polls," the Governor-elect said, "has given me a clear _____ to carry out my program."

18. I had expected a decent tip from the party of six that I waited on early that evening, but all I got was a(n) _____ two bucks!

19. In a series of searing orations, filled with the most _____ language, Cicero launched the full battery of political invective against the hapless Mark Antony.

20. I thought I was unexcitable, but she is as _____ as the granite lions in front of the public library.

21. As soon as I realized that I was wrong, I _____ a public apology for my mistake.

22. In my various _____ through that vast metropolis, I ran across many curious old buildings the ordinary tourist never sees.

Synonyms *Choose the word for this unit that is most nearly **the same** in meaning as each of the following items. Write it in the space given.*

1. irreverent; indecent, lewd; to desecrate _____

2. a novice, beginner, neophyte _____

3. resplendent, luminous, splendid _____

4. to waver, seesaw, fluctuate, oscillate _____

5. measly, meager, piddling, trivial; trashy _____

6. constant, incessant, unrelenting _____

7. abusive, scurrilous, insulting _____

8. nit-picking, hairsplitting, pettifoggery _____

9. a catchphrase, slogan, password _____

10. wary, skittish, cautious; slow to _____

11. a journey, wandering, odyssey _____

12. to defame, slander, libel _____

13. unflappable, unexcitable, serene, unruffled _____

14. evocative, reminiscent; aromatic _____

15. pastoral, rural, rustic _____

16. a fit, convulsion, spasm, seizure _____

17. an increase, accretion, gain _____

18. a dabbler, amateur, trifler _____

19. a conspiracy, plot; connivance, cahoots _____

20. an order, directive _____

21. to offer, present, tender _____

22. an ovation, cheering, plaudits _____

Antonyms   Choose the word for this unit that is most nearly **opposite** in meaning to each of the following items. Write it in the space given.

1. urban, metropolitan _____

2. heedless, reckless, incautious _____

3. excitable, easily upset or flustered _____

4. to withhold, keep back; to accept, receive _____

5. stop-and-go, desultory, intermittent _____

6. complimentary, laudatory, flattering _____

7. a veteran, past master, expert _____

8. unevocative; odorless _____

9. gigantic, immense, colossal _____

10. to forbid, ban, outlaw _____

11. a professional _____

12. to flatter; to whitewash; to praise _____

13. booing, hissing, jeers and catcalls _____

14. a loss; a reduction, decrease _____

15. dim, dark, obscure, dingy, dull, murky _____

16. to remain constant; to be steadfast _____

17. reverent; decent, unsalacious; to hallow _____

Choosing the Right Word   Encircle the **boldface** word that more satisfactorily completes each of the following sentences.

1. How do you have the nerve to offer such a(n) (**paltry, unremitting**) sum for this magnificent "antique" car!

2. Clad in the (**refulgent, bucolic**) armor of moral rectitude, he sallied forth to do battle with the forces of evil.

3. Although he has been in this business for 20 years, he still has the sublime innocence of the most helpless (**tyro, shibboleth**).

4. Since she comes from a rural area, she expresses herself in language that is (**redolent, paltry**) of the farm and country life in general.

5. During the course of my (**peregrinations, paroxysms**) through the world of books, I have picked up all kinds of useful information.

6. It has long been known that some twisted and unhappy people derive a kind of satisfaction from (**calumniating, proffering**) others.

7. Are we to try to make a realistic analysis of our alternatives or let ourselves be distracted by slogans and (**dilettantes, shibboleths**)?

8. Not satisfied with the slow (**increment, peregrination**) of his savings in a bank account, he turned to speculation in the stock market.

9. Perhaps he would be less lyrical about the delights of the (**bucolic, redolent**) life if, like me, he had grown up on a farm in Kansas.

10. The gambler's predictions of the game scores were so incredibly accurate that we suspected some form of (**acclamation, collusion**).

11. I am perfectly willing to listen to a reasonable complaint, but I will not put up with that kind of (**bucolic, vituperative**) backbiting.

12. Once the Senator's nomination became a certainty, all opposition to him evaporated, and he was named by (**vituperation, acclamation**).

13. The phrase "We the people" in the Constitution indicates that the ultimate (**mandate, vacillation**) of our government comes from the popular will.

14. It is easy to criticize him, but how can we overlook the fact that for 20 years he has worked (**unremittingly, charily**) to help the homeless?

15. A (**paroxysm, pedantry**) of indignation flashed through the community, and the streets filled with angry people ready to protest the proposal.

16. Isn't it sheer (**pedantry, refulgence**) on his part to use terms like *Proustian* and *Kafkaesque,* when he knows they mean nothing to his audience?

17. The same difficulties that serve as a challenge to the true professional will be a crushing discouragement to the typical (**mandate, dilettante**).

18. If you continue to (**proffer, profane**) your resignation, there's always a chance that it will be accepted and you'll find yourself out of a job.

19. My objection to the use of (**profane, redolent**) language is not so much that it is vulgar and debasing as that it is weak and inexact.

20. If we (**vacillate, increment**) now at adopting a tough energy policy, we may find ourselves in a desperate situation in the future.

21. I'm not sure if Tom's (**imperturbable, collusive**) spirit is due to toughness or to an inability to understand the dangers of the situation.

22. Because Ms. Montoya is usually so (**chary, imperturbable**) of giving compliments, I felt especially good when she spoke well of my essay.

Review   Units 7–9

Analogies   *In each of the following, choose the item that best completes the comparison.*

1. **bulldozer** is to **raze** as
a. scow is to demolish
b. derrick is to transport
c. truck is to embellish
d. crane is to erect

2. **saturate** is to **water** as
a. calumniate is to steam
b. lubricate is to fire
c. ventilate is to air
d. exacerbate is to oil

3. **imperturbable** is to **fluster** as
a. imperfect is to correct
b. implacable is to appease
c. impulsive is to coerce
d. impressionable is to persuade

4. **felicitous** is to **favorable** as
a. garish is to unfavorable
b. fatuous is to favorable
c. convivial is to unfavorable
d. arrant is to favorable

5. **refulgent** is to **shine** as
a. saturnine is to glow
b. chary is to reek
c. redolent is to smell
d. paltry is to twinkle

6. **tyro** is to **experience** as
a. wraith is to honor
b. counterpart is to status
c. shibboleth is to wisdom
d. dilettante is to seriousness

7. **macabre** is to **horror** as
a. eerie is to terror
b. gruesome is to delight
c. grisly is to panic
d. weird is to discontent

8. **misanthrope** is to **people** as
a. chauvinist is to men
b. pedant is to knowledge
c. xenophobe is to foreigners
d. pacifist is to peace

9. **sneak thief** is to **furtive** as
a. klutz is to adroit
b. showoff is to demure
c. nomad is to stationary
d. hothead is to impetuous

10. **irrefutable** is to **disprove** as
a. immobile is to estimate
b. insuperable is to overcome
c. irascible is to annoy
d. illegible is to write

11. **bucolic** is to **herds** as
a. agrarian is to fields
b. marine is to shores
c. rustic is to clouds
d. urban is to villages

12. **ephemeral** is to **permanence** as
a. erudite is to knowledge
b. grandiose is to scope
c. enormous is to size
d. illusory is to reality

13. **indigent** is to **funds** as
a. jaded is to resources
b. estranged is to attributes
c. orphaned is to parents
d. hackneyed is to friends

14. **raiment** is to **wear** as
a. food is to consume
b. entertainment is to recant
c. money is to counterfeit
d. success is to mandate

15. **unremitting** is to **letup** as
a. unerring is to goal
b. unavailing is to result
c. unflagging is to meaning
d. unpromising is to cause

16. **paltry** is to **quantity** as
a. substantive is to weight
b. gross is to mass
c. perceptive is to insight
d. picayune is to importance

17. **inordinate** is to **restraint** as
a. inconsiderate is to significance
b. indiscriminate is to selectivity
c. intestate is to will power
d. intemperate is to appetite

18. **vituperative** is to **unfavorable** as
a. profane is to favorable
b. substantive is to unfavorable
c. pertinacious is to favorable
d. unremitting is to unfavorable

19. effrontery is to **cheek** as
a. flight is to heel
b. backtalk is to lip
c. peregrination is to foot
d. acclamation is to eye

20. dynamo is to **lackadaisical** as
a. optimist is to saturnine
b. dolt is to fatuous
c. beggar is to indigent
d. bulldog is to pertinacious

Identification   *In each of the following groups, encircle the word that is best defined or suggested by the introductory phrase.*

1. "He seems to do everything in a halfhearted, uninterested way."
a. refulgent   b. profane   c. macabre   d. lackadaisical

2. "The new TV show combines elements from a half dozen other programs."
a. indigent   b. melange   c. pedantry   d. mandate

3. a mirage or a will-o'-the-wisp
a. illusory   b. chary   c. convivial   d. garish

4. the equivalent of our President in a foreign government
a. misanthrope   b. shibboleth   c. tyro   d. counterpart

5. gloomy, serious, and with little to say
a. convivial   b. saturnine   c. bucolic   d. imperturbable

6. the ghost of Hamlet's father
a. coterie   b. wraith   c. raiment   d. slough

7. "Unfortunately, we had to get rid of him to protect our interest."
a. jettison   b. demur   c. portend   d. embellish

8. kept us laughing with their interchange of jokes and quips
a. paucity   b. badinage   c. dilettante   d. litany

9. indications that we may find ourselves in bad trouble
a. calumniate   b. proffer   c. saturate   d. portend

10. look forward to the annual salary increase
a. collusion   b. increment   c. shibboleth   d. dilettante

11. a sudden fit of sobbing that she couldn't control
a. paroxysm   b. acclamation   c. misanthrope   d. slough

12. "Why does he have to show off by quoting from Latin poets!"
a. threshold   b. pedantry   c. echelon   d. paucity

13. just a beginner at tennis
a. counterpart   b. wraith   c. raiment   d. tyro

Shades of Meaning   *Read each sentence carefully. Then encircle the item that best completes the statement below the sentence.*

"Canst thou not minister to a mind diseased,
Pluck from the memory a rooted sorrow,   (2)
Raze out the written troubles of the brain . . . ?"
    (Shakespeare, *Macbeth*, V, 3, 40–42)

1. The phrase **Raze out** in line 3 most nearly means
  a. tear down   c. destroy completely
  b. cut out   d. demolish

R

When the jeep broke down in the middle of the bog, there was nothing left for it but to slough through the mud on foot. **(2)**

2. In line 2 the phrase **slough through** is used to mean
a. cast off
b. shed
c. slog through
d. slither through

The prodigious sums advanced to best-selling authors for tales of murder and mayhem would seem to put the lie to the old shibboleth "Crime doesn't pay." **(2)**

3. The best definition for the word **shibboleth** in line 2 is
a. password
b. custom
c. slogan
d. truism

Though computers have long since eclipsed human beings in the ability to perform complex mathematical calculations, as reasoning entities they are still comparatively bestial. **(2)**

4. The word **bestial** in line 3 most nearly means
a. subhuman in intelligence
b. beastlike
c. depraved and brutal
d. inferior

"O, therefore, love, be of thyself so wary
As I, not for myself, but for thee will; **(2)**
Bearing thy heart, which I will keep so chary
As tender nurse her babe from faring ill." **(4)**
        (Shakespeare, Sonnet 22)

5. In line 3 the word **chary** is used to mean
a. hesitant
b. very close
c. extremely slow with
d. hidden

Antonyms   *In each of the following groups, encircle the word or expression that is most nearly **opposite** in meaning to the **boldface word** in the introductory phrase.*

1. a **furtive** look
a. direct   b. sneaky   c. sorrowful   d. ghostly

2. **razed** the building
a. inspected   b. erected   c. destroyed   d. criticized

3. attempt to **calumniate** one's opponent
a. flatter   b. introduce   c. defame   d. debate

4. a **garish** display
a. inventive   b. exciting   c. tasteless   d. understated

5. **recant** their testimony
a. reaffirm   b. refute   c. condemn   d. forget

6. a **felicitous** turn of phrase
a. apt   b. witty   c. clumsy   d. negative

7. used **profane** language
a. prophetic   b. decent   c. derogatory   d. vulgar

8. proffer assistance
a. lend   b. offer   c. request   d. withhold

9. a **fatuous** comment
a. conceited   b. vapid   c. perceptive   d. surprised

10. due to the **paucity** of supplies
a. dearth   b. abundance   c. destruction   d. arrival

11. an **indigent** community
a. wealthy   b. ethnic   c. poor   d. segregated

12. irrefutable evidence
a. startling   b. disputable   c. unbiased   d. undeniable

13. a **convivial** atmosphere
a. grim   b. salutary   c. sociable   d. mysterious

14. the **acclamation** of the crowd
a. bias   b. cheers   c. jeers   d. departure

15. the **alleged** perpetrator
a. novice   b. veteran   c. bungling   d. proven

Completing the Sentence	*From the following words, choose the one that best completes each of the sentences below. Write the word in the space given.*

Group A

mandate	**saturnine**	**imperturbable**	**paltry**
indigent	**coterie**	**unremitting**	**furtive**

1. How can you in common decency offer me so _____ a sum for four hours of baby-sitting?

2. Only the _____ efforts of all of you, throughout the long, hard campaign, have made possible our great victory in this election.

3. However much it may cost me, I intend to remain true to my principles and obey the _____ of my conscience.

4. Any stranger who moves about in such a(n) _____ way is bound to attract attention and suspicion.

5. The stock market collapse in 1929 cost many wealthy speculators their entire fortunes, leaving them as _____ as paupers.

Group B

saturate	**dilettante**	**bestial**	**illusory**
echelon	**arrant**	**shibboleth**	**bucolic**

1. Before the new brand of toothpaste is launched, the company plans to _____ the market with all kinds of advertising.

2. The _____ charm of this part of New England has attracted many landscape painters seeking to capture the beauties of nature.

3. These famous phrases, expressing the ideals of freedom, have become mere _____ , which people tend to repeat without thinking much about their meaning.

4. Only members of the highest _____ of the State Department were informed of the secret negotiations.

5. "That was no errant curve," punned the veteran sportscaster; "it was a(n) _____ beanball!"

Word Families

A. *On the line provided, write a **noun form** of each of the following words.*

EXAMPLE: allege—**allegation**

1. portend   _____
2. bestial   _____
3. saturate   _____
4. indigent   _____
5. exacerbate   _____
6. refulgent   _____
7. convivial   _____
8. felicitous   _____
9. illusory   _____
10. conciliate   _____
11. vituperative   _____
12. embellish   _____
13. profane   _____
14. vacillate   _____
15. paltry   _____

B. *On the line provided, write a **verb** related to each of the following words.*

EXAMPLE: acclamation — **acclaim**

1. felicitous   _____
2. collusion   _____
3. imperturbable   _____
4. vituperative   _____
5. irrefutable   _____

C. *On the line provided, write an* **adjective** *related to each of the following.*

EXAMPLE: mandate — **mandatory**

1. portend _____

2. misanthrope _____

3. conciliate _____

4. increment _____

5. pedantry _____

**Filling
the Blanks**

Encircle the pair of words that best complete the meaning of each of the following passages.

1. Only a thoroughgoing _____ would enjoy castigating other people's behavior in such unremittingly harsh and _____ language.

a. pedant . . . felicitous
b. misanthrope . . . vituperative
c. tyro . . . profane
d. dilettante . . . convivial

2. The speed with which the Kaiser issued, then _____ , then reissued orders during the crisis was indicative of his essentially weak and _____ personality.

a. embellished . . . pertinacious
b. recanted . . . imperturbable
c. proffered . . . fatuous
d. countermanded . . . vacillating

3. The _____ rains had so _____ the ground over which we passed that it actually squished and gurgled in protest as we trod on it, and our attack had to be postponed until the sun came out again.

a. inordinate . . . razed
b. ephemeral . . . profaned
c. unremitting . . . saturated
d. bestial . . . jettisoned

4. At the June 1961 summit meetings in Vienna President John Kennedy met with his Soviet _____ , Nikita Khrushchev, in an effort to deal with sources of friction between the two superpowers and _____ international fears that the so-called cold war was heating up.

a. counterpart . . . allay
b. raiment . . . mandate
c. coterie . . . exacerbate
d. shibboleth . . . conciliate

5. Though the official is _____ to have been in cahoots with the swindlers, so far no substantive evidence has been brought forward to prove _____ .

a. portended . . . acclamation
b. demurred . . . peregrination
c. alleged . . . collusion
d. calumniated . . . badinage

Analogies   *In each of the following, encircle the letter of the item that best completes the comparison.*

1. tyro is to **neophyte** as
a. wraith is to cadaver
b. suppliant is to recluse
c. misanthrope is to philanthropist
d. agnostic is to skeptic

2. badinage is to **jocular** as
a. acclamation is to pejorative
b. effrontery is to circumspect
c. sarcasm is to mordant
d. sophistry is to felicitous

3. inane is to **fatuous** as
a. plenary is to limited
b. incumbent is to obligatory
c. convivial is to somber
d. utopian is to practical

4. furtive is to **overt** as
a. intermittent is to continuous
b. testy is to irascible
c. indigent is to indignant
d. sumptuous is to lavish

5. reputed is to **alleged** as
a. articulate is to tongue-tied
b. viscous is to dog-tired
c. myopic is to shortsighted
d. prestigious is to old-fashioned

6. juggernaut is to **steamroller** as
a. talisman is to record player
b. maelstrom is to washing machine
c. coterie is to hair drier
d. echelon is to vacuum cleaner

7. increment is to **more** as
a. deduction is to less
b. debit is to more
c. asset is to less
d. decrease is to more

8. carping is to **picayune** as
a. sophistry is to irrefutable
b. exigency is to optional
c. verbiage is to inordinate
d. nuance is to egregious

9. nettle is to **conciliate** as
a. raze is to allay
b. exacerbate is to ramify
c. embellish is to portend
d. mandate is to countermand

10. vacillate is to **temporize** as
a. calumniate is to slander
b. eschew is to embrace
c. hallow is to desecrate
d. jettison is to salvage

Shades of Meaning   *Read each sentence carefully. Then encircle the item that best completes the statement below the sentence.*

"Do not embrace me till each circumstance
Of peace, time, fortune, do cohere and jump
That I am Viola. . . ."   (Shakespeare, *Twelfth Night*, V, 1, 256–260)   (2)

1. The word **cohere** in line 2 is used to mean
a. stick together
b. make a whole
c. have meaning
d. recognize one another

Behind the facade of a respectable repair shop there hid a fencing operation, and what passed for customers were in fact petty thieves bringing their furtive goods to barter for cash.   (2)

2. In line 3 the word **furtive** most nearly means
a. sneaky   b. stealthy   c. shifty   d. stolen

"The rest to some faint meaning make pretense,
But Shadwell never deviates into sense."
    (John Dryden, "MacFlecknoe," 19–20)   (2)

3. The best definition for the word **deviates** in line 2 is
a. strays   b. differs   c. sneaks   d. corrupts

Bowing to the unbending realities of political deal making, the freshman
legislator abandoned his hard-line stance and pronounced himself
ready to temporize. **(2)**

4. The word **temporize** in line 3 most nearly means
   a. stall   b. filibuster   c. compromise   d. procrastinate

"Still to ourselves in every place consigned,
Our own felicity we make or find. **(2)**
With secret course, which no loud storms annoy,
Glides the smooth current of domestic joy." **(4)**
        (Samuel Johnson, "Lines Added to Goldsmith's Traveller")

5. The word **felicity** in line 2 is best defined as
   a. apposition   b. happiness   c. good taste   d. aptness

**Filling
the Blanks**
*Encircle the pair of words that best complete the
meaning of each of the following passages.*

1. Even though he had been educated by the foremost philosopher of his
   age, the emperor Nero possessed the _____ mind and
   _____ appetites of a monster like Count Dracula or the
   Marquis de Sade.
   a. meretricious . . . refulgent   c. murky . . . prepossessing
   b. fecund . . . piquant   d. depraved . . . bestial

2. As the speaker grew more heated, his address began to turn into an
   intemperate _____ , chock-full of the most scathing and
   _____ abuse I have ever been "privileged" to hear.
   a. diatribe . . . vituperative   c. malediction . . . taciturn
   b. eulogy . . . incendiary   d. indictment . . . halcyon

3. In my various _____ through the forest that bordered on my
   childhood home, I often came quite unexpectedly upon birds, insects, and
   other _____ creatures that I had never before encountered.
   a. paroxysms . . . bucolic   c. peregrinations . . . sylvan
   b. gambits . . . macabre   d. pedantries . . . mundane

4. I realized that my theory about how the crime had been committed was no
   longer _____ when I accidentally stumbled across
   _____ evidence of a quite different scenario.
   a. coherent . . . moot   c. ludicrous . . . substantive
   b. tenable . . . irrefutable   d. abject . . . indubitable

5. Any trial that is being conducted by people with absolutely no sense of
   _____ can only be considered a _____
   of justice.
   a. equity . . . travesty   c. concord . . . counterpart
   b. propriety . . . figment   d. collusion . . . bastion

Unit 10

Definitions   *From the words in Group A and Group B following, choose the one that most nearly corresponds to each definition below. Write the word in the space at the right of the definition and in the illustrative phrase below it.*

Group A

askance (ə 'skans)
attenuate (ə 'ten yü āt)
benign (bi 'nīn)
cavil ('kav əl)
charlatan ('shär lə tən)
concatenation (kän kat ə 'nā shən)

concomitant (kən 'käm ə tənt)
decimate ('des ə māt)
foible ('foi bəl)
forgo (fôr 'gō)
fraught (frôt)

1. (*adj.*) full of or loaded with; accompanied by
   _____ with danger   _____

2. (*adj.*) gentle, kind; forgiving, understanding; having a favorable or beneficial effect; not malignant
   a(n) _____ influence   _____

3. (*v.*) to make thin or slender; to weaken or lessen in force, intensity, or value
   took steps to _____ the pain   _____

4. (*v.*) to find fault in a petty way, carp; (*n.*) a trivial objection or criticism
   _____ at imperceptible flaws   _____

5. (*n.*) a weak point, failing, minor flaw
   the _____ of humanity   _____

6. (*n.*) one who feigns knowledge or ability; a pretender, impostor, or quack
   expose the _____   _____

7. (*adj.*) accompanying; occurring concurrently; (*n.*) something that accompanies another thing
   since disease is the natural _____ of poverty   _____

8. (*adv.*) with suspicion, mistrust, or disapproval
   look _____ at the suggestion   _____

9. (*v.*) to kill or destroy a large part of
   _____ the enemy's forces   _____

10. (*n.*) a linking together in a sequence; a chain
    the _____ of events   _____

11. (*v.*) to do without, abstain from, give up
    _____ dessert   _____

Group B

inure (in 'yür)
luminous ('lü mə nəs)
obsequious (əb 'sē kwē əs)
obtuse (äb 'tüs)
oscillate ('äs ə lāt)
penitent ('pen ə tənt)

peremptory (pə 'remp tə rē)
rebuff (ri 'bəf)
reconnoiter (rē kə 'noit ər)
shambles ('sham bəlz)
sporadic (spô 'rad ik)

12. (n.) a slaughterhouse; a place of mass bloodshed; a state of complete disorder and confusion _____

made a(n) _____ of the office

13. (adj.) having the nature of a command that leaves no opportunity for debate, denial, or refusal; offensively self-assured, dictatorial; determined, resolute _____

a(n) _____ tone of voice

14. (v.) to toughen, harden; to render used to something by long subjection or exposure _____

_____ to hardship

15. (adj.) regretful for one's sins or mistakes; (n.) one who is sorry for wrongdoing _____

was sincerely _____

16. (adj.) marked by slavish attentiveness; excessively submissive, often for purely self-interested reasons _____

_____ courtiers

17. (adj.) occurring at irregular intervals, having no set plan or order _____

_____ gunfire

18. (v.) to snub; to repel, drive away; (n.) a curt rejection; a check, setback _____

_____ their offer of help

19. (v.) to engage in reconnaissance; to make a preliminary inspection _____

_____ the terrain

20. (v.) to swing back and forth with a steady rhythm; to fluctuate or waver _____

watched the pendulum _____

21. (adj.) emitting or reflecting light, glowing; illuminating _____

a night _____ with starlight

22. (adj.) blunt, not coming to a point; slow or dull in understanding; measuring between 90° and 180°; not causing a sharp impression _____

too _____ to see the danger

Completing the Sentence *Choose the word for this unit that best completes each of the following sentences. Write it in the space given.*

1. The general sent scouts on ahead of the army to _____ the area for a suitable site to pitch camp.

2. In one horrible moment, the airplane crash converted the quiet streets of that suburban community into a ghastly _____ .

3. Good supervisors know that they can get more cooperation from their staff by making polite requests than by issuing _____ orders.

4. The man's personality was a strange mixture of strengths and weaknesses, fortes and _____ .

5. Any "investment counselor" who promises to double your money overnight must be regarded as a(n) _____ or a crook.

6. Though my childhood recollections have been _____ by the passage of time, they have not been totally effaced from my memory.

7. Though critics _____ at minor faults in the new Broadway show, the general public loved the piece.

8. Life on the family farm has _____ me to hard physical labor and long hours of unremitting toil.

9. Although there had been some _____ fighting earlier, the real battles of the Civil War did not begin until Bull Run in July, 1861.

10. I find it absolutely incredible that such a bizarre _____ of improbabilities could actually lead to the outbreak of a major war.

11. During imperial times, the Roman Senate was little more than a collection of _____ yes-men, intent upon preserving their own lives by gratifying the emperor's every whim.

12. His statements have been so uniformly _____ that I get the impression that he is wearing a permanent pair of mental blinders.

13. As all kinds of wild rumors ran rampant through the besieged city, the mood of the populace _____ between hope and despair.

14. During the 14th century, the Black Death suddenly swept across Europe, _____ the population and paralyzing everyday life.

15. No doubt he's very sorry he got caught, but that does not mean that he's at all _____ about what he did.

16. I think *The World Turned Upside Down* is an apt title for any study of war and its _____ social and economic dislocations.

17. Although the moon appears to be a(n) _____ body, the fact is that it only reflects light received from the sun.

18. In a typical James Bond movie, Agent 007 has a series of adventures that are _____ with tongue-in-cheek peril.

19. Unless the title Special Aide to the Assistant Section Manager involves a salary increase, I would just as soon _____ it.

20. I was relieved to learn that the tumor on my arm was _____ and my worst fears groundless.

21. We look _____ at any program that makes it harder for city dwellers to get out and enjoy the beauties of nature.

22. I was totally taken aback when they _____ my kind offers of assistance so rudely and nastily.

Synonyms *Choose the word for this unit that is most nearly **the same** in meaning as each of the following items. Write it in the space given.*

1. to fluctuate, waver, vibrate, vacillate _____

2. remorseful, regretful, rueful, sorry _____

3. fawning, servile, sycophantic, mealymouthed _____

4. to thin out, dilute, water down _____

5. a shortcoming, failing, flaw, defect, quirk _____

6. radiant, bright, refulgent, lustrous _____

7. to nitpick, quibble, carp _____

8. to ravage, wreak havoc, devastate _____

9. dull-witted, stupid, dumb, thick; mild _____

10. irregular, intermittent, spasmodic _____

11. to harden, accustom, acclimate _____

12. to spurn, repulse, reject; a setback _____

13. a series, sequence, conjunction _____

14. benevolent, salutary, salubrious _____

15. a mess, disaster area; a slaughterhouse _____

16. to do without, refrain from, renounce _____

17. a fraud, quack, mountebank, impostor _____

18. attendant, accompanying, corollary _____

19. high-handed, dictatorial; unconditional _____

20. full of, loaded with, charged with _____

21. distrustfully, suspiciously, skeptically _____

22. to scout, see how the land lies _____

Antonyms *Choose the word for this unit that is most nearly **opposite** in meaning to each of the following items. Write it in the space given.*

1. a person's strong suit, forte; a virtue _____

2. devoid of, lacking, deficient in _____

3. assertive, bumptious; overbearing; candid, frank; independent _____

4. unrepentant, remorseless, uncontrite _____

5. constant, steady, continuous, uninterrupted _____

6. irresolute, tentative; mild, unassuming _____

7. acute, perceptive, quick-witted _____

8. to indulge in, partake of _____

9. the real McCoy, genuine article _____

10. to thicken; to strengthen, bolster _____

11. dark, opaque, dim, murky _____

12. to remain fixed, steady, or constant _____

13. malignant; malevolent, deleterious _____

14. to accept, take someone up on, welcome _____

Choosing the Right Word *Encircle the **boldface** word that more satisfactorily completes each of the following sentences.*

1. During the Civil War the ranks of both armies were (**decimated, rebuffed**) as much by disease as by enemy action.

2. Since he didn't want to give me credit for having done a good job, he took refuge in endless (**foibles, cavils**) about my work.

3. Since he is not guided by firm principles, he (**attenuates, oscillates**) between the rival factions, looking for support from both of them.

4. Lack of consideration for other people is an unfortunate (**charlatan, concomitant**) of her driving ambition.

5. When I found that people I admired were looking (**askance, sporadic**) at my unconventional clothing, I resolved to remedy the situation.

6. I have learned that (**sporadic, peremptory**) sessions of intense "cramming" can never take the place of a regular study program.

7. All angles are classified as acute, right, (**obtuse, benign**), or straight, according to the number of degrees they contain.

8. Imagine the general disappointment when the so-called "miracle cure" was exposed as a fraud promoted by a (**charlatan, cavil**).

9. We must never allow our passion for justice to be (**inured, attenuated**) to mere halfhearted goodwill.

10. Do you want to be a ballet dancer badly enough to (**oscillate, forgo**) those fattening foods you love so much?

11. Their relationship has been so (**fraught, benign**) with strife and malice that I don't see how they can ever patch things up.

12. We believe that classes taught by teachers with specialized training will have a (**sporadic, benign**) effect on the troubled children.

13. Bank robbers often spend a good deal of time (**reconnoitering, rebuffing**) the neighborhood in which the bank they intend to rob is located.

14. Though Americans are always ready to settle a conflict peacefully, they are not afraid to use (**luminous, peremptory**) force when necessary.

15. How could you have the heart to (**rebuff, cavil**) those people's piteous appeals for aid?

16. By a happy (**shambles, concatenation**) of events, the right boy, the right girl, and the right music came together on the dance floor that night.

17. Over the years, her (**luminous, obtuse**) explanations and scintillating wit have helped her students master the difficult subject she taught.

18. At an autocrat's court, free speech is usually replaced by the (**penitent, obsequious**) twaddle of self-serving flunkies and toadies.

19. Though I admire the woman's strong points, I find her (**rebuffs, foibles**) laughable.

20. The (**concomitant, penitent**) youths agreed to work without pay until they could make restitution for the damage their carelessness had caused.

21. Even though my experiences in battle have (**inured, caviled**) me to scenes of suffering, I was horrified by the devastation wrought by the tornado.

22. Somehow or other, a bull got into the china shop and turned it into a complete (**shambles, concatenation**).

Unit 11

Definitions

From the words in Group A and Group B following, choose the one that most nearly corresponds to each definition below. Write the word in the space at the right of the definition and in the illustrative phrase below it.

Group A

abrogate ('ab rə gāt)
ambient ('am bē ənt)
asperity (a 'sper ə tē)
burnish ('bər nish)
cabal (kə 'bal)
delectable (di 'lek tə bəl)

deprecate ('dep rə kāt)
desuetude ('des wə tüd)
detritus (di 'trīt əs)
ebullient (i 'bůl yənt)
eclectic (e 'klek tik)

1. (v.) to make smooth or glossy by rubbing, polish; (n.) gloss, brightness, luster

_____

_____ a brass candlestick

2. (adj.) overflowing with enthusiasm and excitement; boiling, bubbling

_____

in a(n) _____ mood

3. (adj.) delightful, highly enjoyable; deliciously flavored, savory; (n.) an appealing or appetizing food or dish

_____

a truly _____ dish

4. (v.) to repeal, cancel, declare null and void

_____

_____ a treaty

5. (n.) roughness, severity, bitterness, or tartness

_____

the _____ of the criticism

6. (n.) loose bits and pieces of material resulting from disintegration or wearing away; fragments that result from any destruction

_____

in the _____ of the landslide

7. (n.) disuse, the state of being discontinued

_____

fallen into _____

8. (adj.) completely surrounding

_____

the _____ air

9. (n.) a small group working in secret

_____

the members of the _____

10. (v.) to express mild disapproval; to belittle

_____

_____ such foolish practices

11. (adj.) drawn from different sources; (n.) one whose beliefs are drawn from various sources

_____

a(n) _____ style of architecture

Group B

emanate (′em ə nāt)
flaccid (′flas əd, ′flak səd)
impecunious (im pə ′kyü nē əs)
inexorable (in ′ek sər ə bəl)
moribund (′môr ə bənd)
necromancer (′nek rə man sər)

onerous (′än ər əs)
rife (rīf)
rudiments (′rüd ə mənts)
sequester (si ′kwes tər)
winnow (′win ō)

12. (*v.*) to set apart, separate for a special purpose; to take possession of and hold in custody

_____

_____ funds pending a court decision

13. (*adj.*) dying, on the way out

_____

a(n) _____ custom

14. (*n.*) one who claims to reveal or influence the future through magic, especially communication with the dead; in general, a magician or wizard

_____

resorted to _____ and sorcerers

15. (*v.*) to get rid of something unwanted, delete; to sift through to obtain what is desirable; to remove the chaff from wheat by blowing air on it; to blow on, fan

_____

_____ out inaccuracies

16. (*adj.*) limp, not firm; lacking vigor or effectiveness

_____

_____ muscles

17. (*adj.*) common, prevalent, happening often; full, abounding; plentiful, abundant

_____

since rumors were _____

18. (*adj.*) inflexible, beyond influence; relentless, unyielding

_____

a(n) _____ fate

19. (*adj.*) burdensome, oppressive; involving hardship or difficulty

_____

a(n) _____ duty

20. (*v.*) to proceed or come forth from some point of origin, issue, originate; to send forth

_____

rays that _____ from the sun

21. (*adj.*) having little or no money

_____

in my present _____ state

22. (*pl. n.*) the parts of any subject or discipline that are learned first; the earliest stages of anything

_____

the _____ of chess

Completing the Sentence

Choose the word for this unit that best completes each of the following sentences. Write it in the space given.

1. All the facts and figures point to one _____ conclusion: we are hopelessly outnumbered.

2. Some superstitious Roman emperors consulted _____ and other dabblers in black magic to find out what the future held.

3. There is nothing more _____ on a hot day than to stretch out in a hammock with a good book and a pitcher of icy lemonade!

4. The copper pots had been so highly _____ that I could see my face in them.

5. Even before they said a word, I could tell from their _____ faces that our team had won.

6. We will never allow anyone to curtail or _____ the basic rights and liberties guaranteed to us in the Constitution.

7. In order to prevent outside influences from coming into play, a jury is normally _____ until it reaches a decision.

8. One of Darwin's theories suggests that nature ensures the survival of a species by slowly _____ out the less fit members.

9. When our volleyball coach gives her pregame pep talk, the enthusiasm that _____ from her sparks our whole team.

10. It is often difficult to hold a conversation while walking on a busy city street because of the high level of _____ traffic noise.

11. It was then that he began to organize the _____ that would later depose the king.

12. She is a very private person who _____ any attempt to honor publicly her great services to humanity.

13. In a sense, the man is a(n) _____ philosopher because his ideas have been influenced by many different schools of thought.

14. As air slowly seeped out through the tiny puncture, the inner tube became more and more _____ .

15. I could tell that my boss was really "riled" by the _____ of his tone of voice when he summoned me.

16. Though the institution of monarchy still exists in some parts of the world, it is more or less a(n) _____ form of government.

17. I thought the job of revising the manuscript would be a relatively simple matter, but it proved to be a(n) _____ task.

18. The conversation at dinner tables all over town was _____ with speculation as to the outcome of the big game.

19. The plot of the novel centers on a(n) _____ adventurer who attempts to remedy his financial embarrassment by marrying into money.

20. Recalcitrant students used to be beaten into submission, but such barbarous practices have long since fallen into _____ .

21. Late that night, we began the heartbreaking task of sifting through the _____ of the explosion looking for victims.

22. Unless you have mastered the _____ of French grammar, you will find it difficult to speak the language fluently.

Synonyms *Choose the word for this unit that is most nearly **the same** in meaning as each of the following items. Write it in the space given.*

1. penniless, impoverished, indigent _____

2. to sift, strain, filter, sort out _____

3. to deplore, frown upon, look askance at _____

4. to originate, issue; to emit, give off _____

5. to seclude, segregate, isolate, closet _____

6. inescapable, ineluctable; obdurate _____

7. selective, synthetic, pick-and-choose _____

8. a clique, ring, gang; a plot, conspiracy _____

9. exhilarated, elated, exuberant _____

10. a sorcerer, conjurer, wizard _____

11. to polish, shine, buff _____

12. dying, on the wane, obsolescent _____

13. rigor, severity, harshness, roughness _____

14. disuse, discontinuance, neglect _____

15. delightful, delicious, enjoyable _____

16. soft, flabby, limp _____

17. fundamentals, basics, first principles _____

18. burdensome, oppressive _____

19. to annul, revoke, cancel _____

20. debris, wreckage, ruins, rubble   _____

21. widespread, prevalent; abundant   _____

22. encompassing, surrounding   _____

Antonyms   *Choose the word for this unit that is most nearly* ***opposite*** *in meaning to each of the following items. Write it in the space given.*

1. mildness, blandness, softness, lenity   _____

2. to smile on, countenance, approve   _____

3. all of a piece, uniform, monolithic   _____

4. firm, hard, solid   _____

5. flourishing, thriving, on the rise   _____

6. the fine points   _____

7. to tarnish, dull; to abrade   _____

8. use; existence; prevalence   _____

9. affluent, wealthy, prosperous, rich   _____

10. light, easy, undemanding, untaxing   _____

11. avoidable; yielding, pliant   _____

12. to reaffirm, renew; to ratify   _____

13. repugnant, repulsive, distasteful   _____

14. to absorb, soak up, draw in, attract   _____

15. devoid of, lacking, scarce as hen's teeth   _____

16. gloomy, morose, sullen; apathetic, blasé   _____

Choosing the Right Word   *Encircle the* ***boldface*** *word that more satisfactorily completes each of the following sentences.*

1. "The (**inexorable, moribund**) march of the years," said the aged speaker, "decrees that this is the last time I will address you."

2. Though the presidency confers great powers on the person who holds the office, it also saddles that person with (**onerous, eclectic**) responsibilities.

3. As we sat in the locker room after our heartbreaking loss, the (**ambient, impecunious**) gloom was so thick you could almost cut it.

4. What appeared to be an informal study group was in reality a highly organized (**detritus, cabal**) determined to overthrow the government.

5. Oliver Wendell Holmes, Jr., once observed that he did not wish to lead a(n) (**sequestered, abrogated**) life, far from the conflicts of his times.

6. You may be sure that any directive that (**abrogates, emanates**) from her office will be clear, precise, and workable.

7. When I retire, I will be embarking on a challenging new phase of my life, not entering a period of "innocuous (**desuetude, asperity**)."

8. Writing that is so full of soggy clichés, gummy sentence structure, and excessive wordiness can best be described as (**inexorable, flaccid**).

9. (**Asperity, Necromancy**) and other forms of witchcraft were punishable by death during the Middle Ages.

10. Though she entered this country as a(n) (**impecunious, rife**) child, she eventually made a fortune in the garment industry.

11. (**Eclectic, Ambient**) schools of art are typical of a period when there is little original inspiration or bold experimentation.

12. Since archeologists spend a lot of time rummaging through the (**detritus, desuetude**) of vanished civilizations, they bear a striking resemblance to junk collectors and ragpickers.

13. It is one thing to (**burnish, deprecate**) human follies and pretensions; it is quite another to correct them.

14. The old adage that "one man's meat is another man's poison" simply means that what is considered (**delectable, onerous**) is often quite subjective.

15. The (**moribund, burnished**) helmets and breastplates of the warriors gleamed and twinkled in the morning sunlight.

16. The charm of this musical comedy lies in its slam-bang pacing, its sprightly music, and its generally (**onerous, ebullient**) good cheer.

17. No one, however powerful or dominant, can (**abrogate, emanate**) the basic moral laws on which civilization rests.

18. As one veteran aptly observed, a soldier had to be hardy to cope with the (**asperities, cabals**) of life in the trenches during World War I.

19. Any political party that is (**rife, ebullient**) with petty jealousies and back-biting can never hope to present a united front in an election.

20. Though skeptics insist that patriotism is (**onerous, moribund**) in America, I believe that it is alive and well in the hearts of the people.

21. Anyone who has the slightest acquaintance with the (**rudiments, cabals**) of economics understands that we cannot solve our financial problems simply by borrowing more and more money.

22. The investigating committee spent long hours trying to (**burnish, winnow**) fact from fiction in the witnesses' testimony.

Unit 12

Definitions *From the words in Group A and Group B following, choose the one that most nearly corresponds to each definition below. Write the word in the space at the right of the definition and in the illustrative phrase below it.*

Group A

aesthetic (es 'thet ik)
conjecture (kən 'jek chər)
defunct (di 'fəŋkt)
discomfit (dis 'kəm fit)
espouse (es 'paůz)
fetish ('fet ish)

gregarious (grə 'gâr ē əs)
hapless ('hap lis)
impeccable (im 'pek ə bəl)
importune (im pôr 'tyün)
interpolate (in 'tər pə lāt)

1. (*v.*) to trouble with demands; to beg for insistently

   _____

   _____ us for a loan

2. (*n.*) an object believed to have magical powers; an object of unreasoning devotion or reverence

   _____

   currently a popular _____

3. (*v.*) to take up and support; to become attached to, adopt; to marry

   _____

   _____ a program of reform

4. (*v.*) to insert between other parts or things; to present as an addition or correction

   _____

   _____ lines into the script

5. (*adj.*) living together in a herd or group; sociable, seeking the company of others

   _____

   an outgoing and _____ person

6. (*adj.*) pertaining to beauty; sensitive or responsive to beauty, artistic

   _____

   a purely _____ concern

7. (*v.*) to frustrate, thwart, or defeat; to confuse, perplex, or embarrass

   _____

   _____ one's enemies

8. (*adj.*) marked by persistent absence of good luck

   _____

   the _____ victim of a practical joke

9. (*n.*) a guess, tentative theory; (*v.*) to make a guess, surmise

   _____

   merely _____ at this point

10. (*adj.*) faultless, beyond criticism or blame

    _____

    _____ taste in clothing

11. (*adj.*) no longer in existence or functioning, dead _____

   a(n) _____ organization

Group B

irreparable (i ′rep ər ə bəl)	**perfunctory** (per ′fəŋk tə rē)
laconic (lə ′kän ik)	**plaintive** (′plān tiv)
languish (′laŋ gwish)	**requite** (ri ′kwīt)
mendacious (men ′dā shəs)	**tantamount** (′tan tə maúnt)
nadir (′nā dər)	**unregenerate** (ən ri ′jen ə rət)
omnipresent (äm ni ′pre zənt)	

12. (*adj.*) concise, using few words _____

   a(n) _____ statement

13. (*n.*) the lowest point _____

   the _____ of his popularity

14. (*v.*) to become weak, feeble, or dull; to droop; to be
depressed or dispirited; to suffer neglect _____

   _____ for years in prison

15. (*adj.*) incapable of being repaired or rectified _____

   do _____ harm

16. (*adj.*) done in a superficial or halfhearted manner;
without interest or enthusiasm _____

   a(n) _____ search

17. (*adj.*) given to lying or deception; untrue _____

   a(n) _____ account of the affair

18. (*adj.*) present in all places at all times _____

   a(n) _____ deity

19. (*adj.*) equivalent, having the same meaning, value, or
effect _____

   _____ to a declaration of war

20. (*v.*) to make suitable repayment, as for a kindness,
service, or favor; to make retaliation, as for an injury
or wrong; to reciprocate _____

   was handsomely _____ for my services

21. (*adj.*) expressive of sorrow or woe, melancholy _____

   in a(n) _____ tone of voice

22. (*adj.*) persisting in holding obstinately to old ideas or
habits; unrepentant, unreformed _____

   a(n) _____ scoundrel

12

Completing the Sentence   *Choose the word for this unit that best completes each of the following sentences. Write it in the space given.*

1. As his irrepressible flow of reminiscences continued without a letup, I tried in vain to _____ a few observations of my own.

2. One wall of the museum was filled with charms and _____ designed to ward off everything from a hangnail to the evil eye.

3. Last night, Central High's Netnicks captured the basketball championship by _____ the South High Slammers, 61 to 44.

4. Responding to the melancholy note in the song of the nightingale, Keats wrote of its "_____ anthem."

5. I was greatly relieved to learn that the accident I had with my car last week didn't do any _____ damage to the motor.

6. When asked what terms he would offer the Confederate army, General Grant made the _____ reply, "Unconditional surrender!"

7. Every general seems to have one defeat that marks the _____ of his military fortunes—for example, Lee at Gettysburg or Grant at Cold Harbor.

8. Since extroverts are _____ by nature, they usually prefer not to live alone.

9. Since the coroner's findings were inconclusive, the exact cause of death must remain for the present a matter of _____ .

10. "Don't you think it's a little foolish to pursue the young lady when your warm feelings for her are clearly not _____ ?" I asked.

11. When you get more experience on the job, you will learn that a "request" from your employer is _____ to an order.

12. From a(n) _____ point of view, the painting didn't appeal to me, but I kept it because it was a memento of my childhood.

13. Never once has the least whiff of scandal or impropriety tainted the man's _____ reputation as an upstanding member of this agency.

14. It's easy enough to back a popular program, but it takes real courage to _____ a cause that most people oppose.

15. No sooner did the _____ old reprobate get out of jail than he returned to the life of crime that got him there in the first place.

16. I felt a little foolish when the librarian told me that I was asking for the current issue of a magazine that had long been _____ .

17. The _____ creature had somehow gotten its foot caught in the grate and could not extricate it without help.

18. Suddenly I was surrounded by a mob of grubby little street urchins loudly _____ me for a handout.

19. I thought our state legislators would consider the proposal at the earliest opportunity, but they let it _____ in committee for months.

20. They claim to have made a thorough search of the premises, but I suspect that their efforts were no more than _____ .

21. To say that he is _____ does not even begin to convey just how alienated he is from any regard for the truth.

22. No matter where candidates for high political office go these days, the _____ eye of the TV camera seems focused on them.

Synonyms   *Choose the word for this unit that is most nearly **the same** in meaning as each of the following items. Write it in the space given.*

1. to implore, entreat; to dun, tax   _____

2. slapdash, cursory, superficial, shallow   _____

3. to insert, inject, interpose, introduce   _____

4. equivalent to, indistinguishable from   _____

5. flawless, spotless, immaculate   _____

6. relating to beauty, artistic   _____

7. unlucky, ill-starred, unfortunate   _____

8. to droop, flag, wilt, fade; to pine   _____

9. rock bottom, the lowest point   _____

10. to nonplus, disconcert; to foil, thwart; to rout   _____

11. unreformed, unreconstructed; stubborn   _____

12. to embrace, adopt, take up   _____

13. sociable, outgoing, extroverted   _____

14. terse, succinct, pithy, compact   _____

15. lying, untruthful; false   _____

16. a charm, talisman; an obsession   _____

17. extinct, nonexistent, dead   _____

18. sad, doleful, melancholy, lugubrious _____

19. to reimburse, recompense, repay; to avenge _____

20. ubiquitous, ever-present _____

21. to speculate, surmise; a supposition _____

22. irremediable, beyond repair _____

Antonyms   Choose the word for this unit that is most nearly
opposite in meaning to each of the following items.
Write it in the space given.

1. alive and well, extant; in effect _____

2. lucky, fortunate, charmed _____

3. truthful, veracious _____

4. introverted, reclusive, aloof _____

5. grimy, soiled, spotted, sullied _____

6. reformed; penitent, remorseful _____

7. fixable, reversible, remediable _____

8. cheerful, blithe, joyous, merry _____

9. thorough, assiduous, diligent, meticulous _____

10. to repudiate, disavow, renounce _____

11. a known fact, a certainty, a surety _____

12. garrulous, prolix, loquacious, verbose _____

13. the apex, pinnacle, zenith _____

Choosing the   Encircle the **boldface** word that more satisfactorily
Right Word   completes each of the following sentences.

1. Though I left the house feeling "as fit as a fiddle," my spirits began to
(**requite, languish**) after only five minutes in that withering heat.

2. One of the comforting things about reaching the (**fetish, nadir**) of one's
career is that the only place to go from there is up.

3. Although fate has decreed that he make his living as a stockbroker, his
main interests and talents are definitely (**irreparable, aesthetic**).

4. One of the best-known figures of American folklore is the lean, tough,
(**laconic, hapless**) cowboy.

5. I don't know which is more painful—to have to ask someone for a favor, or to have some unfortunate (**importune, discomfit**) one for help.

6. Perhaps we can't change the minds of (**unregenerate, plaintive**) racists, but we can stop them from translating their prejudices into public policy.

7. The legal adage "Silence implies consent" means that not objecting to an action that concerns you is (**perfunctory, tantamount**) to approving it.

8. "Since I don't have enough hard evidence to say for sure," the detective said, "I can only (**requite, conjecture**) that this was an inside job."

9. Many scholars believe that Beaumont or Fletcher (**interpolated, requited**) a scene or two into the present text of Shakespeare's *Macbeth*.

10. Fortunately, our lawyer was able to produce documents that disproved the (**mendacious, omnipresent**) assertions of our former partner.

11. The sternness of my boss's expression so (**discomfited, languished**) me that at first I had difficulty responding to the question.

12. The (**omnipresent, gregarious**) threat of a nuclear holocaust that characterized the Cold War era changed many people's attitudes toward war in profound and permanent ways.

13. It is one thing to be concerned about discipline; it is quite another to make a (**conjecture, fetish**) of it.

14. Though few of us today stand on ceremony to quite the extent that our ancestors did, common courtesy is by no means (**unregenerate, defunct**).

15. Then she sang a (**laconic, plaintive**) little ditty about a man who yearns wistfully for the girl he left behind many years before.

16. A diplomat must always proceed on the assumption that no rupture between nations, no matter how serious, is (**irreparable, perfunctory**).

17. Prehistoric peoples banded together into tribes, not only for protection, but also to satisfy their (**gregarious, mendacious**) instincts.

18. In our desire to improve the quality of life in America, we should not be too quick to (**importune, espouse**) an idea simply because it is new.

19. When the scandal broke, the man found himself the (**hapless, impeccable**) victim of his own lies and deceit.

20. Perhaps we should be overjoyed that the great man condescended to give us a(n) (**aesthetic, perfunctory**) nod as we passed by.

21. Her sense of tact is so (**hapless, impeccable**) and unerring that she can handle the most trying situation as if it were mere child's play.

22. I hope to (**espouse, requite**) my parents with more than mere respect for all the care and love they have showered on me.

Review Units 10–12

Analogies   *In each of the following, choose the item that best completes the comparison.*

1. impeccable is to **fault** as
a. indispensable is to correct
b. intangible is to estimate
c. inedible is to grow
d. irreparable is to fix

2. liar is to **mendacious** as
a. judge is to perfunctory
b. extrovert is to gregarious
c. villain is to benign
d. convict is to unregenerate

3. defunct is to **dead** as
a. inexorable is to thriving
b. extant is to lively
c. moribund is to dying
d. delectable is to alive

4. rife is to **number** as
a. fraught is to quantity
b. sporadic is to size
c. concomitant is to scope
d. tantamount is to texture

5. necromancer is to **dead** as
a. palmist is to tarot cards
b. astrologer is to stars
c. wizard is to tea leaves
d. ventriloquist is to birds

6. onerous is to **bear** as
a. eclectic is to prove
b. portable is to carry
c. vulnerable is to wound
d. cumbersome is to handle

7. penitent is to **remorse** as
a. jubilant is to grief
b. crestfallen is to relief
c. plaintive is to woe
d. serene is to anger

8. hapless is to **luck** as
a. impecunious is to money
b. gregarious is to friends
c. patriotic is to country
d. ambidextrous is to skill

9. charlatan is to **genuine** as
a. turncoat is to perfidious
b. pickpocket is to adroit
c. recluse is to aloof
d. ignoramus is to knowledgeable

10. aesthetics is to **beauty** as
a. ethics is to structure
b. phonetics is to history
c. semantics is to meaning
d. metaphysics is to form

11. obtuse is to **discernment** as
a. flaccid is to firmness
b. peremptory is to speed
c. ebullient is to enthusiasm
d. omnipresent is to occurrence

12. beggar is to **importune** as
a. millionaire is to extort
b. banker is to embezzle
c. philanthropist is to sequester
d. creditor is to dun

13. scout is to **reconnoiter** as
a. saboteur is to construct
b. watchdog is to guard
c. derelict is to map
d. surveyor is to demolish

14. inexorable is to **relent** as
a. adamant is to yield
b. craven is to flee
c. complaisant is to please
d. timid is to shrink

15. luminous is to **light** as
a. onerous is to smell
b. querulous is to taste
c. sonorous is to sound
d. unctuous is to color

16. chamois is to **burnish** as
a. clothespin is to polish
b. sponge is to press
c. towel is to heat
d. steel wool is to scour

17. attenuate is to **slender** as
a. elongate is to wide
b. curtail is to short
c. expand is to thin
d. dilate is to tall

18. ebullient is to **bubble** as
a. delectable is to foam
b. sporadic is to froth
c. turbulent is to seethe
d. halcyon is to boil

19. toady is to **obsequious** as
a. fetish is to reliable
b. miser is to avaricious
c. jester is to plaintive
d. charlatan is to hapless

20. laconic is to **length** as
a. sluggish is to celerity
b. trenchant is to acuity
c. luminous is to clarity
d. concise is to brevity

Identification   *In each of the following groups, encircle the word that is best defined or suggested by the introductory phrase.*

1. an artillery barrage that took a heavy toll of life and limb
a. cavil   b. decimate   c. sequester   d. importune

2. exposed as an utter fraud
a. shambles   b. charlatan   c. desuetude   d. defunct

3. how fate may sometimes be characterized
a. inexorable   b. aesthetic   c. perfunctory   d. ambient

4. given to trivial and frivolous objections
a. attenuate   b. forgo   c. reconnoiter   d. cavil

5. "At that moment, life seemed more hopeless than it ever has before or since."
a. conjecture   b. cabal   c. nadir   d. gregarious

6. getting used to cold weather before going on the camping trip
a. inure   b. espouse   c. winnow   d. luminous

7. suffering an unbroken string of bad breaks and disappointments
a. delectable   b. benign   c. obtuse   d. hapless

8. "Each event led to a result, which in turn caused another event."
a. concatenation   b. oscillate   c. askance   d. flaccid

9. learning the basic strokes, moves, and tactics of tennis
a. rudiments   b. concomitant   c. foibles   d. eclectic

10. genuinely sorry for one's mistakes
a. obsequious   b. ebullient   c. interpolate   d. penitent

11. will never undertake anything without his "lucky coin" with him
a. fetish   b. rife   c. luminous   d. concatenation

12. lessened the impact of the economic recession
a. conjecture   b. impecunious   c. rebuff   d. attenuate

13. "I think this forced inactivity is making me a useless wreck."
a. discomfit   b. fraught   c. desuetude   d. asperity

14. a minor, often humorous failing
a. requite   b. foible   c. abrogate   d. detritus

15. a small group that plotted to oust me from the club presidency
a. oscillate   b. cabal   c. onerous   d. deprecate

16. regard his suggestions with deep suspicion
a. defunct   b. askance   c. plaintive   d. laconic

17. never happy unless she has a lot of people around her
a. peremptory   b. irreparable   c. moribund   d. gregarious

18. humbling himself in an effort to be accepted by the class leaders
a. languish   b. obsequious   c. nadir   d. mendacious

19. a type of wizard or warlock
a. omnipresent   b. emanate   c. necromancer   d. unregenerate

20. laden with
a. sporadic   b. fraught   c. tantamount   d. impeccable

Shades of Meaning   *Read each sentence carefully. Then encircle the item that best completes the statement below the sentence.*

By the end of 1864 Southern war-making resources were so far depleted that Confederate commanders could hope to do no more than deal temporary rebuffs to the inexorable Union juggernaut.   (2)

1. In line 3 the word **rebuffs** is best defined as
a. curt rejections   c. snubs
b. cease-fires   d. setbacks

"What peremptory eagle-sighted eye
    Dares look upon the heaven of her brow,   (2)
That is not blinded by her majesty?"
        (Shakespeare, *Love's Labour's Lost,* IV, 3, 226–228)

2. The word **peremptory** in line 1 most nearly means
a. dictatorial   b. unconditional   c. resolute   d. rude

The mad scientist, a stock character in Hollywood B movies of the 1950s, is often found in a dark laboratory, surrounded by a sinister array of test tubes, retorts, and beakers of ebullient potions.   (2)

3. The best definition for the word **ebullient** in line 3 is
a. boiling   b. enthusiastic   c. delicious   d. poisoned

"When from our better selves we have too long
Been parted by the hurrying world, and droop,   (2)
Sick of its business, of its pleasures tired,
How gracious, how benign, is Solitude."   (4)
        (Wordsworth, *The Prelude*)

4. In line 4 the word **benign** is used to mean
a. forgiving   b. salutary   c. benevolent   d. lonely

The deep hush was broken when a gust of wind billowed through the parlor window and winnowed the pages of the book that lay open on the table.   (2)

5. The word **winnowed** in line 2 most nearly means
a. deleted   b. sorted out   c. tore   d. fanned

The infamous Hatfield-McCoy feud began in earnest when, in 1882, the Hatfields requited the slaying of Ellison Hatfield by executing three McCoy brothers.   (2)

6. In line 2 the word **requited** is used to mean
a. avenged   b. recompensed   c. reimbursed   d. witnessed

Antonyms   In each of the following groups, encircle the word or expression that is most nearly **opposite** in meaning to the word in **boldface type** in the introductory phrase.

1. a **moribund** industry
   a. dying   b. depressed   c. flourishing   d. controversial

2. **sporadic** fighting
   a. fitful   b. continuous   c. bloody   d. mock

3. an **obtuse** comment
   a. frightening   b. perceptive   c. comical   d. foolish

4. **deprecate** their pranks
   a. approve   b. describe   c. contrive   d. condemn

5. **forgo** dessert
   a. indulge in   b. concoct   c. refrain from   d. serve

6. **abrogate** the agreement
   a. renew   b. debate   c. nullify   d. reveal

7. **espouse** a military solution
   a. devise   b. select   c. repudiate   d. support

8. a **benign** growth
   a. malignant   b. attractive   c. harmless   d. familiar

9. **irreparable** damage
   a. fatal   b. instant   c. unforeseen   d. reversible

10. **flaccid** leadership
    a. weak   b. energetic   c. new   d. elected

11. served a **delectable** punch
    a. delicious   b. powerful   c. traditional   d. repulsive

12. **rebuff** their advances
    a. spurn   b. expect   c. welcome   d. question

13. an **onerous** task
    a. burdensome   b. easy   c. supplementary   d. obligatory

14. an **impecunious** relative
    a. impoverished b. close   c. wealthy   d. kindly

15. surprised by the **asperity** of the remarks
    a. mildness   b. severity   c. length   d. candor

16. **eclectic** tastes
    a. selective   b. weird   c. creative   d. uniform

17. a **mendacious** witness
    a. deceitful   b. convincing   c. unwilling   d. truthful

18. a **laconic** reply
    a. humorous   b. verbose   c. concise   d. sarcastic

19. a **plaintive** tone of voice
    a. doleful   b. loud   c. joyful   d. sorrowful

20. **burnish** the silver plate
    a. tarnish   b. melt   c. polish   d. steal

**Completing
the Sentence**

*From the following lists of words, choose the one that
best completes each of the sentences below. Write the
word in the appropriate space.*

Group A

abrogate	discomfit	winnow	hapless
ambient	eclectic	fetish	perfunctory
emanate	nadir	shambles	sporadic

1. In less than a minute, the tragic accident converted the factory into a ghastly _____ .

2. He was like a small island of integrity in the _____ ocean of corruption and deceit.

3. A sense of peace and spiritual strength seemed to _____ from the interior of the old church.

4. Her _____ literary style shows the influence of many writers, ranging from the 18th century to the present day.

5. My employer's _____ manner of greeting me each morning gave me the impression that he was scarcely aware of my existence.

6. The would-be burglars were thoroughly _____ by the store's elaborate security system and were forced to give up their attempt to break in.

Group B

obtuse	impeccable	tantamount	interpolate
cabal	decimate	rudiments	unregenerate
obsequious	languish	foible	oscillate

1. "How can you expect to play in a championship tournament when you haven't yet mastered the _____ of the game?" I asked incredulously.

2. Though I admire your strong points, I find your _____ somewhat amusing.

3. It is never too late for even the most _____ sinner to repent and regain moral and spiritual well-being.

4. Failure to hand in your term paper on time is _____ to accepting a failing grade for the course.

5. Allow me at this point to _____ a few remarks that I think will clarify the situation for all of us.

6. I was horrified when I dropped an order of lobster, complete with butter sauce, all over that _____ white suit!

7. Disease had so thoroughly _____ the invader's army that it was forced to halt all operations and withdraw from the field.

Word Families

A. *On the line provided, write a* **noun form** *of each of the following words.*

EXAMPLE: attenuate—**attenuation**

1. oscillate _____
2. abrogate _____
3. requite _____
4. sequester _____
5. discomfit _____
6. impeccable _____
7. emanate _____
8. deprecate _____
9. gregarious _____
10. obtuse _____
11. mendacious _____
12. omnipresent _____
13. ambient _____
14. inexorable _____
15. ebullient _____
16. espouse _____
17. decimate _____
18. interpolate _____
19. flaccid _____
20. plaintive _____

B. *On the line provided, write a* **verb** *related to each of the following words.*

EXAMPLE: discomfiture—**discomfit**

1. conjectural _____
2. espousal _____
3. irreparable _____
4. unregenerate _____
5. concatenation _____

C. *On the line provided, write an* **adjective** *related to each of the following words.*

EXAMPLE: oscillate — **oscillatory**

1. deprecate _____
2. conjecture _____
3. importune _____
4. penitence _____
5. luminosity _____

Filling the Blanks   *Encircle the pair of expressions that best complete the meaning of each of the following passages.*

1. The "truth-in-advertising" laws that many states have recently passed were in part designed to discourage crooks and _____ from making _____ claims about the products they offer to the unsuspecting public.
   - a. charlatans . . . mendacious
   - b. necromancers . . . sporadic
   - c. fetishes . . . laconic
   - d. cabals . . . eclectic

2. Though Seneca embraced the tenets of Stoicism in their entirety, Cicero _____ no one school of Greek philosophy, but, like a true _____ , chose what he thought best from each and ignored the rest.
   - a. discomfited . . . penitent
   - b. abrogated . . . aesthetic
   - c. espoused . . . eclectic
   - d. deprecated . . . foible

3. Though the man appeared to be the most _____ pauper on the face of the earth, he had actually _____ large sums of money in various hiding places in the hovel he called home.
   - a. flaccid . . . burnished
   - b. impecunious . . . sequestered
   - c. ambient . . . interpolated
   - d. benign . . . decimated

4. As soon as I heard its _____ cries for help, I knew that the _____ animal had once again got its paw caught in the grillwork on the front porch.
   - a. obsequious . . . moribund
   - b. laconic . . . impeccable
   - c. onerous . . . defunct
   - d. plaintive . . . hapless

5. Although many of the pioneers found it difficult at first to cope with the _____ of frontier life, they were a hardy race, who quickly became _____ such rough-and-tumble living.
   - a. rudiments . . . importuned by
   - b. asperities . . . inured to
   - c. concomitants . . . decimated by
   - d. shambles . . . discomfited by

Analogies *In each of the following, choose the item that best completes the comparison.*

1. **indigent** is to **impecunious** as
   a. furtive is to overt
   b. halcyon is to turbulent
   c. hapless is to unfortunate
   d. felicitous is to awkward

2. **sporadic** is to **intermittent** as
   a. brackish is to fresh
   b. ephemeral is to transitory
   c. fraught is to devoid
   d. utopian is to feasible

3. **miser** is to **sequester** as
   a. misanthrope is to invest
   b. neophyte is to filch
   c. agnostic is to embezzle
   d. spendthrift is to squander

4. **omnipresent** is to **ubiquitous** as
   a. moribund is to obsolescent
   b. laconic is to garrulous
   c. extant is to extinct
   d. eclectic is to monolithic

5. **carp** is to **cavil** as
   a. decry is to deprecate
   b. conciliate is to nettle
   c. hallow is to profane
   d. espouse is to eschew

6. **acuity** is to **obtuse** as
   a. perspicacity is to myopic
   b. equity is to impartial
   c. credence is to gullible
   d. asperity is to harsh

7. **luminous** is to **refulgent** as
   a. ebullient is to saturnine
   b. murky is to lucid
   c. verdant is to arid
   d. redolent is to aromatic

8. **hypocrite** is to **dissemble** as
   a. charlatan is to feign
   b. suppliant is to sham
   c. wraith is to simulate
   d. counterpart is to conceal

9. **pendulum** is to **oscillate** as
   a. clock is to temporize
   b. scale is to portend
   c. wave is to undulate
   d. wheel is to ramify

10. **surveillance** is to **monitor** as
    a. espionage is to overlook
    b. vigilance is to sleep
    c. sabotage is to pacify
    d. reconnaissance is to reconnoiter

Shades of Meaning *Read each sentence carefully. Then encircle the item that best completes the statement below the sentence.*

Physicists employ gigantic devices called particle accelerators to smash atoms together at tremendous velocities in order to investigate the primordial nature of matter. (2)

1. The word **primordial** in line 3 most nearly means
   a. earliest   b. fundamental   c. primeval   d. original

The movie is cracked up to be a scathing indictment of the fashion industry, but I could detect very little sting in it at all. On the contrary, its effect, to my mind, was rather obtuse. (2)

2. In line 3 the word **obtuse** is used to mean
   a. blunt   b. thick   c. dumb   d. mild

A blockbuster movie or a best-selling novel often spawns a host of usually paltry imitations cranked out by those opportunist hacks whose eyes are ever turned to the main chance. (2)

3. The best definition for the word **paltry** in line 2 is
   a. despicable   b. mean   c. measly   d. inferior

I am at a loss to judge whether her self-deprecating manner bespeaks
genuine humility or false modesty.   (2)

4. The word **self-deprecating** in line 1 is best defined as
    a. self-belittling   c. self-assured
    b. self-critical   d. self-serving

> "Such smiling rogues as these,
> Like rats, oft bite the holy cords a-twain   (2)
> Which are too intrinse t'unloose; smooth every passion . . .
> Renege, affirm, and turn their halcyon beaks   (4)
> With every gale and vary of their masters,
> Knowing nought, like dogs, but following."   (6)
>   (Shakespeare, *King Lear,* II, 2, 79–81, 84–86)

5. In line 4 the word **halcyon** is used to mean
    a. peaceful   b. kingfisher   c. prosperous   d. happy

**Filling
the Blanks**   *Encircle the pair of words that best complete the
meaning of each of the following passages.*

1. After the bulldozers and wrecking balls had completed the lengthy task of
_____ the building, a convoy of dump trucks began the job
of carting off the resultant _____ .
    a. embellishing . . . flotsam   c. razing . . . detritus
    b. belaboring . . . desuetude   d. exhuming . . . largesse

2. The _____ antics of the troupe of clowns convulsed the
audience. _____ of laughter repeatedly shook the hall like
salvos of musketry.
    a. fatuous . . . Gambits   c. feckless . . . Bastions
    b. ludicrous . . . Paroxysms   d. inane . . . Litanies

3. For two solid hours, our artillery kept up a(n) _____ barrage
of cannon fire. It _____ the enemy's ranks with such deadly
accuracy that barely one man in ten was left alive after it was over.
    a. unremitting . . . decimated   c. inexorable . . . atrophied
    b. unregenerate . . . winnowed d. illusory . . . enervated

4. Since all the members of my little _____ of friends truly
enjoy each other's company, our weekly get-togethers are remarkably
_____ affairs.
    a. covenant . . . vituperative   c. concatenation . . . gregarious
    b. cabal . . . meretricious   d. coterie . . . convivial

5. The poor man had been _____ in the Bastille and left
to _____ there without hope of reprieve for over
twenty years.
    a. mandated . . . demur   c. inured . . . exacerbate
    b. incarcerated . . . languish   d. garnered . . . vacillate

Unit 13

Definitions   *From the words in Group A and Group B following, choose the one that most nearly corresponds to each definition below. Write the word in the space at the right of the definition and in the illustrative phrase below it.*

Group A

abstruse (ab 'strüs)
affront (ə 'frənt)
canard (kə 'närd)
captious ('kap shəs)
cognizant ('käg ni zənt)
contrite (kən 'trīt)

cynosure ('sī nə shür)
decorous ('dek ər əs)
deign (dān)
desiccated ('des ə kā tid)
efficacy ('ef ə kə sē)

1. (*adj.*) aware, knowledgeable, informed

   made me _____ of my rights

2. (*v.*) to think it appropriate or suitable to one's dignity to do something; to condescend

   _____ to speak to us

3. (*adj.*) regretful for some misdeed or sin; plagued by a sense of guilt; thoroughly penitent

   the look of one who is truly _____

4. (*adj.*) extremely difficult to understand

   a(n) _____ theory

5. (*n.*) a false rumor, fabricated story

   spread a ridiculous _____

6. (*adj.*) well behaved, dignified, socially proper

   act in a(n) _____ manner

7. (*n.*) the power to produce a desired result

   the _____ of the remedy

8. (*n.*) the center of attraction, attention, or interest; something that serves to guide or direct

   the _____ of all eyes

9. (*n.*) an open or intentional insult; a slight; (*v.*) to insult to one's face; to face in defiance, confront

   a(n) _____ to our dignity

10. (*adj., part.*) thoroughly dried out; divested of spirit or vitality; arid and uninteresting

    slowly _____ by the sun

11. (*adj.*) excessively ready to find fault; given to petty criticism; intended to trap, confuse, or show up

    a(n) _____ critic

Group B

engender (in 'jen dər)
ethereal (i 'thēr ē əl)
facade (fə 'säd)
ghoulish ('gül ish)
incongruous (in 'kän grü əs)
machination (mak ə 'nā shən)

mesmerize ('mez mə rīz)
opprobrium (ə 'prō brē əm)
preempt (prē 'empt)
putative ('pyü tə tiv)
simplistic (sim 'plis tik)

12. (n.) a crafty, scheming, or underhanded action
designed to accomplish some (usually evil) end

_____

the victim of his rival's _____

13. (v.) to seize upon to the exclusion of others, take over
or appropriate; to be presented in place of, displace

_____

_____ the best seats

14. (n.) the front or face of a building; a surface
appearance (as opposed to what may lie behind)

_____

the _____ of the cathedral

15. (adj.) light, airy, delicate; highly refined; suggesting
what is heavenly (rather than earthbound)

_____

the _____ beauty of an angel

16. (adj.) generally regarded as such; reputed;
hypothesized, inferred

_____

the _____ origin of the custom

17. (n.) disgrace arising from shameful conduct, infamy;
contempt, reproach

_____

the _____ that attaches to a traitor's name

18. (adj.) highly oversimplified, simpleminded

_____

a(n) _____ view of a problem

19. (v.) to hypnotize; to fascinate, enthrall

_____

_____ the audience

20. (v.) to bring into existence, give rise to, produce;
to come into existence, assume form

_____

_____ interest in the program

21. (adj.) revolting in an unnatural or morbid way;
suggestive of someone who robs graves or
otherwise preys on the dead

_____

a(n) _____ practice

22. (adj.) not in keeping, unsuitable, incompatible

_____

made a decidedly _____ couple

Completing   *Choose the word for this unit that best completes each*
the Sentence   *of the following sentences. Write it in the space given.*

1. After the battle, camp followers began the _____ process of stripping the dead of whatever valuables they possessed.

2. The _____ of the unscrupulous wheeler-dealers involved in that unsavory scandal boggle the imagination.

3. The pages of the old book were so _____ that they began to crumble as soon as we touched them.

4. Am I supposed to feel honored simply because that arrogant lout sometimes _____ to nod vaguely in my direction?

5. The longer I study this country's history, the more _____ I become of my rich heritage of freedom.

6. For more than five minutes she stared at the telegram containing the bad news, as if she were _____ .

7. At the risk of appearing a trifle _____ , I would like to raise a few small objections to the wording of this proposal.

8. To be the _____ of all eyes could be the joyous fulfillment of a dream or the unhappy realization of a nightmare.

9. Some teachers are able to present the most _____ subjects in terms that are crystal-clear to even the dullest of students.

10. Some historians question whether Benedict Arnold really deserves all the _____ he has been accorded as America's arch-traitor.

11. Unfortunately, the complex problems facing today's world cannot be solved by recourse to an overly _____ notion of good and evil.

12. Only a thoroughly naive and gullible person would actually believe every preposterous _____ that circulates in this school.

13. I didn't really believe that he was sorry for what he had done until I saw the _____ expression on his sad little face.

14. What could be more _____ than the 6-foot, 7-inch center on the basketball team dolled up in baby clothes for the class play!

15. There is now a vast body of evidence that supports the idea that poverty tends to _____ crime.

16. The cherubic faces and _____ voices of the choristers almost made me believe that the music they were singing was coming from heaven.

17. The only surefire way to establish the _____ of a new drug in treating a disease is to test it "in the field."

18. His fantastic stories about his academic, athletic, financial, and romantic achievements are a(n) _____ to common sense.

19. Except for a balcony built during the Truman administration, the _____ of the White House has remained virtually unchanged since it was constructed.

20. No one knows for sure who really wrote the scene, but Shakespeare is generally regarded as its _____ author.

21. A TV network will sometimes _____ its regularly scheduled programming to air special broadcasts of national interest.

22. The child's conduct during the ceremony may not have been appropriately _____ , but it wasn't horrendous either.

Synonyms   *Choose the word for this unit that is most nearly **the same** in meaning as each of the following items. Write the word in the space provided.*

1. the focus of attention, focal point   _____

2. dehydrated, shriveled, parched   _____

3. to take over, commandeer, appropriate   _____

4. incompatible, discordant, jarring   _____

5. the front, exterior, surface; a mask, pretense   _____

6. seemly, becoming, tasteful, dignified   _____

7. to hypnotize; to bewitch, entrance   _____

8. dishonor, infamy, odium, shame, disgrace   _____

9. to see fit, deem; to condescend, stoop   _____

10. an insult, slight, offense; to offend   _____

11. fiendish; barbarous, monstrous   _____

12. remorseful, penitent, rueful   _____

13. esoteric, arcane, recondite, occult   _____

14. a plot, scheme, maneuver, dirty trick   _____

15. oversimplified, simpleminded   _____

16. aware of, conscious of; acquainted with   _____

17. to beget, generate, cause; to form   _____

18. heavenly, celestial; airy, gossamer   _____

19. a false story, wild rumor, hoax   _____

20. faultfinding, nit-picking, carping   _____

21. reputed, supposed, presumed   _____

22. effectiveness, potency, reliability   _____

Antonyms   _Choose the word for this unit that is most nearly **opposite** in meaning to each of the following items. Write it in the space given._

1. unaware of, unconscious of, oblivious of   _____

2. a compliment, praise; to praise   _____

3. sodden, soggy, waterlogged, drenched   _____

4. infernal, hellish; thick, heavy   _____

5. acclaim, honor, glory, renown   _____

6. easily grasped, simple, straightforward   _____

7. unseemly, unbecoming, improper, tasteless   _____

8. unrepentant, unapologetic, impenitent   _____

9. compatible, harmonious, consistent   _____

10. overly complicated or complex   _____

11. ineffectiveness, impotence   _____

12. to stop, put an end to; to deter   _____

13. uncritical, not given to carping   _____

14. known, corroborated, confirmed   _____

15. the interior, what lies beneath the surface   _____

Choosing the Right Word   _Encircle the **boldface** word that more satisfactorily completes each of the following sentences._

1. The audience was so quiet after the curtain fell that I couldn't tell whether they were bored or (**deigned, mesmerized**) by her artistry.

2. His unmistakable interest in the gruesome details of the tragedy revealed that he possessed the sensibilities of a (**canard, ghoul**).

3. Her quiet speech, subdued clothes, and (**decorous, desiccated**) manner made it hard to believe that she was the famous rock star.

4. He tried to conceal his lack of scholarship and intellectual depth by using unnecessarily (**efficacious, abstruse**) language.

5. The candidate's "shocking revelation" about his opponent was later shown to be nothing more than a malicious (**canard, cynosure**).

6. I resent your nasty question about whether or not I will "(**deign, affront**) to speak to ordinary students" after I'm elected class president.

7. The book describes in great detail the odious (**machinations, facades**) involved in Adolf Hitler's rise to power in Germany.

8. The President must always be on his toes because a careless answer to a (**contrite, captious**) question could land him in political hot water.

9. Why should we go out for the school show when we know that all the good roles have been (**engendered, preempted**) by Seniors?

10. He acts like someone whose vital juices have long since dried up, leaving only a drab and (**desiccated, contrite**) shell behind.

11. For any actor, it is a unique thrill to know that when you are alone on stage, you are the (**facade, cynosure**) of hundreds of pairs of eyes.

12. It has been said that humor is essentially the yoking of (**incongruous, ethereal**) elements within a familiar or recognizable framework.

13. Philologists believe that many Western languages can be traced back to a (**putative, decorous**) parent tongue known as Indo-European.

14. Unfortunately, the vexed question of their rights in this matter does not admit of a (**ghoulish, simplistic**) solution.

15. In my youthful folly, I inadvertently (**affronted, preempted**) the very people whose aid I was attempting to enlist.

16. The (**efficacy, opprobrium**) of history forever attaches itself to the name of Lee Harvey Oswald, the assassin of President Kennedy.

17. "Do we have sufficient evidence at hand," I asked, "to judge the (**efficacy, cognizance**) of the new method of teaching reading?"

18. A government that fails to bring about peaceful reform (**engenders, deigns**) the kind of social unrest that makes violent revolution inevitable.

19. Like many people who are completely wrapped up in themselves, she simply isn't (**cognizant, decorous**) of the larger world around her.

20. The play is so peopled with spirits and other incorporeal beings that it has the (**ethereal, captious**) quality of a dream.

21. If you had listened to my warnings in the first place, there would be no need for you to feel (**contrite, desiccated**) now.

22. It wasn't at all hard to recognize signs of extreme uneasiness beneath her (**canard, facade**) of buoyant optimism.

Unit 14

Definitions   *From the words in Group A and Group B following, choose the one that most nearly corresponds to each definition below. Write the word in the space at the right of the definition and in the illustrative phrase below it.*

Group A

beatific (bē ə 'tif ik)
behemoth (bi 'hē məth)
blandishment ('blan dish mənt)
cacophonous (kə 'käf ə nəs)
chicanery (shi 'kā nə rē)
complaisant (kəm 'plā sənt)

consign (kən 'sīn)
coup (kü)
euphemism ('yü fə miz əm)
febrile ('feb ril)
gainsay ('gān sā)

1. (*adj.*) feverish; pertaining to or marked by fever   _____

   _____ activity

2. (*n.*) a mild or inoffensive expression used in place of a harsh or unpleasant one   _____

   simply a(n) _____ for *die*

3. (*adj.*) obliging, wanting to please or serve others   _____

   a(n) _____ assistant

4. (*adj.*) harsh-sounding, discordant   _____

   _____ laughter

5. (*n.*) a creature of enormous size, power, or appearance   _____

   whales, the " _____ of the deep"

6. (*v.*) to deny, contradict; to dispute   _____

   _____ a conclusion

7. (*n., often pl.*) anything designed to flatter or coax; sweet talk, apple-polishing   _____

   the subtle _____ of a sycophant

8. (*n.*) trickery, deceptive practices or tactics   _____

   indulge in legal _____

9. (*adj.*) blissful; rendering or making blessed   _____

   a positively _____ expression on her face

10. (*v.*) to give over to another's care, charge, or control; to entrust, deliver; to set apart for a special use   _____

    _____ their names to oblivion

11. (*n.*) a highly successful stroke, act, plan, or stratagem   _____

    the _____ that toppled the government

Group B

imminent ('im ə nənt)	**nostrum** ('näs trəm)
innate (i 'nāt)	**pariah** (par 'ī ə)
loath (lōth)	**replete** (ri 'plēt)
manifest ('man ə fest)	**visionary** ('vizh ə ner ē)
minutiae (mə 'nü shē ē)	**wizened** ('wiz ənd)
moratorium (môr ə tōr ē əm)	

12. (*pl. n.*) small or trivial details, trifling matters _____

  too concerned with _____

13. (*n.*) a suspension of activity; an official waiting
period; an authorized period of delay _____

  a(n) _____ on arms sales

14. (*adj.*) filled to capacity; provided in abundance _____

  a life _____ with honor

15. (*n.*) an alleged cure-all; a remedy or scheme of
questionable effectiveness _____

  quacks peddling _____ to the ignorant

16. (*adj., part.*) dry, shrunken, and wrinkled (often as the
result of aging) _____

  laid a(n)_____ hand on my shoulder

17. (*adj.*) natural, inborn, inherent; built-in _____

  a(n) _____ talent

18. (*n.*) an outcast; one who is rejected by a social group
or organization _____

  when lepers were shunned as _____

19. (*adj.*) about to happen, threatening _____

  because a storm was _____

20. (*adj.*) unwilling, reluctant, disinclined _____

  _____ to retire at sixty-five

21. (*adj.*) not practical, lacking in realism; having the
nature of a fantasy or dream; (*n.*) one given to
far-fetched ideas _____

  see with the eyes of a(n) _____

22. (*adj.*) clear, evident to the eyes or mind; (*v.*) to show
plainly, exhibit, evince; (*n.*) a list of cargo and/or
passengers _____

  "_____ Destiny"

118

Completing the Sentence *Choose the word for this unit that best completes each of the following sentences. Write it in the space given.*

1. If you spend all your time on _____ , you won't have any left for really important matters.

2. Since I was brought up in a sleepy country town, I found it very hard to adjust to the _____ pace of big-city life.

3. The nation's economic ills call for a variety of remedies; they cannot be cured by any single, miraculous _____ .

4. She is a delightful woman whose conversation is _____ with wry witticisms, penetrating observations, and interesting allusions.

5. On the first play, our diminutive quarterback was "sacked" by a veritable _____ of a linebacker, ominously nicknamed "Bone Crusher."

6. One way to bring relief to small farmers who cannot meet their mortgage payments is to declare a temporary _____ on foreclosures.

7. We had expected him to be tough and hostile in the negotiations, but he proved to be _____ almost to a fault.

8. No matter what _____ you use to describe his conduct, you can't disguise the fact that he betrayed his best friend.

9. Though the ability to paint is probably a(n) _____ gift, it can certainly be improved by training and practice.

10. Before you dismiss him as just another impractical _____ , think of how many great inventors were once regarded as mere "cranks."

11. Only a fool would have succumbed to the cloying _____ of that smooth-talking rascal!

12. Some Civil War generals weren't professional soldiers and got their jobs through wire-pulling and other forms of political _____ .

13. Some people enjoy the type of atonal music written by such composers as Arnold Schoenberg; others find it _____ .

14. We were all surprised that someone with the reputation of a frivolous playboy could _____ such courage and determination.

15. Though her body had become bent and _____ with age, her mind was as alert and active as ever.

16. You may be, as you say, "_____ to leave such a fascinating book," but I'm telling you right now to take out the garbage!

17. Suddenly I was overcome by such a feeling of _____ peace that I began to wonder whether I was on earth or in heaven.

18. When it became clear just how shamelessly he had treated his brother, he became a virtual _____ in his own family.

19. However much I may dispute your views, I will never _____ your right to hold them.

20. When the swollen river threatened to overflow its banks, a devastating flood seemed _____ .

21. In a touching ceremony, the soldiers _____ the body of their fallen leader to the grave and his memory to their hearts.

22. Just when it seemed that defeat was inevitable, she pulled off a dazzling _____ that totally discomfited her opponent.

Synonyms   *Choose the word for this unit that is most nearly **the same** in meaning as each of the following items. Write the word in the space provided.*

1. a postponement, delay, stoppage   _____

2. inborn, inherent, intrinsic, congenital   _____

3. averse, reluctant, indisposed, disinclined   _____

4. to exhibit, reveal, disclose; apparent   _____

5. a panacea, cure-all, elixir   _____

6. trivia, trifles, minor details   _____

7. withered, shriveled, dried up, wrinkled   _____

8. to dispute, deny, controvert, contradict   _____

9. utopian, idealistic; impractical   _____

10. impending, looming, threatening   _____

11. an allurement, enticement; cajolery   _____

12. bursting, bristling, filled   _____

13. sharp practice, double-dealing, trickery   _____

14. obliging, accommodating, eager to please   _____

15. an outcast, untouchable, persona non grata   _____

16. blissful, rapturous, ecstatic, transcendent   _____

17. a masterstroke, tour de force   _____

18. a milder substitute for a harsh or unpleasant expression   _____

19. harsh-sounding, raucous, dissonant   _____

20. feverish, frenetic   _____

21. a mammoth, whale, elephant, colossus   _____

22. to transfer, deliver, remit, convey   _____

Antonyms   *Choose the word for this unit that is most nearly* ***opposite*** *in meaning to each of the following items. Write it in the space given.*

1. a dwarf, pygmy, midget   _____

2. willing, eager, inclined   _____

3. realistic, practical, down-to-earth   _____

4. harmonious, melodious, mellifluous   _____

5. a blunder, faux pas, gaffe   _____

6. distant, remote, faraway   _____

7. to hide, conceal; unrevealed, hidden   _____

8. devoid, empty, barren, lacking   _____

9. bloated, distended   _____

10. disconsolate, dejected, doleful   _____

11. uncooperative, unobliging, insubordinate   _____

12. leisurely, relaxed, "laid-back"   _____

13. major issues or concerns; the overall picture   _____

14. learned, acquired; extrinsic, accidental   _____

15. ethical practices, fair dealings   _____

16. to confirm, corroborate, support   _____

17. an acceleration; an escalation   _____

18. a threat, intimidation, strong-arm tactic   _____

Choosing the Right Word   *Encircle the* ***boldface*** *word that more satisfactorily completes each of the following sentences.*

1. How could a novel so (**replete, visionary**) with interesting situations, believable characters, and stimulating ideas fail to be popular?

2. The solution to our problems is to be found in long-term programs of social planning, not in easy (**pariahs, nostrums**).

3. The (**complaisant, febrile**) tempo of the symphony's opening movement gives way to a placid and stately largo in the next.

4. Accidents at nuclear power plants have prompted some people to agitate for a (**moratorium, nostrum**) on the construction of such facilities.

5. After it had been left to rot in the sun for a few days, the plump little apple began to take on the (**visionary, wizened**) appearance of a prune.

6. The plan is certainly ingenious, but it strikes me as far too (**visionary, imminent**) to serve as the basis for practical legislation.

7. After he killed Alexander Hamilton in a duel, Aaron Burr found himself no longer a respected statesman, but a social and political (**coup, pariah**).

8. Someone who "can't see the woods for the trees" is usually too concerned with (**minutiae, nostrums**) to be aware of the overall picture.

9. "The evidence that we will present in this trial," the prosecutor told the jury, "will make the defendant's guilt abundantly (**beatific, manifest**)."

10. The two of them are so unfailingly sweet and (**imminent, complaisant**) that I sometimes find their personalities a little cloying.

11. No one who knows the facts would venture to (**gainsay, consign**) your claim to have done your utmost to improve this community.

12. Only when we tried to implement the plan did its (**innate, complaisant**) defects become clear to us.

13. Although I am (**febrile, loath**) to boast, I must acknowledge my superior qualities as a student, athlete, financier, and all-round social luminary.

14. "How much of a chance do you suppose a 98-pound weakling like me actually stands against that 320-pound (**coup, behemoth**)?" I asked incredulously.

15. When he took his first bite of Mother's famous coconut custard pie, a look of (**replete, beatific**) joy spread over his face.

16. (**Imminent, Loath**) disaster stared us in the face when we were thrown for a loss and then fumbled the ball on our own five-yard line.

17. It is a rare leader indeed who can tell the public unpleasant truths without evasions or (**pariahs, blandishments**).

18. The (**cacophony, moratorium**) that suddenly greeted my ears made me suspect that a fox had somehow gotten into the henhouse.

19. "As soon as we received the order," I said, "we crated the equipment and (**gainsaid, consigned**) it to the buyer in Atlanta."

20. It didn't make me any happier to learn that my firing was being referred to (**euphemistically, cacophonously**) as a "termination."

21. Although I play a fair hand of bridge, I'm not capable of the brilliant (**coups, manifests**) that mark a true master of the game.

22. The kind of financial (**minutiae, chicanery**) involved in bringing off that deal may not have been illegal, but it was certainly unethical.

Unit 15

Definitions *From the words in Group A and Group B following, choose the one that most nearly corresponds to each definition below. Write the word in the space at the right of the definition and in the illustrative phrase below it.*

Group A

affectation (af ek 'tā shən)
amenity (ə 'men ə tē)
aperture ('ap ər chər)
dissidence ('dis ə dəns)
epicurean (ep ə 'kyü rē ən)
improvident (im 'präv ə dənt)

iniquity (i 'nik wə tē)
inviolable (in 'vī ə lə bəl)
mutable ('myü tə bəl)
nascent ('nā sənt)
obeisance (ō 'bē səns)

1. (*adj.*) sacred; of such character that it must not be broken, injured, or profaned   _____

    a(n) _____ trust

2. (*n.*) a difference of opinion; discontent   _____

    _____ in the ranks

3. (*n.*) a deep bow or other body movement indicating respect or submission; deference, homage   _____

    make a(n) _____ before a king

4. (*adj.*) devoted to the pursuit of pleasure; fond of good food, comfort, and ease; with discriminating tastes; (*n.*) a person with discriminating tastes   _____

    a(n) _____ delight

5. (*n.*) pleasantness; that which is pleasant or agreeable; (*pl.*) attractive features, customs, etc.   _____

    observe the social _____

6. (*adj.*) open to or capable of change, fickle   _____

    as _____ as fashion

7. (*adj.*) not thrifty; failing to plan ahead   _____

    a(n) _____ spendthrift

8. (*n.*) an opening, gap, hole   _____

    through the _____ in the wall

9. (*n.*) a habit or mannerism assumed for effect; a pretentious display of manners or sentiments that are not genuine   _____

    a ludicrously sophomoric _____

10. (*adj.*) just beginning to exist or develop; having just come into existence   _____

    _____ opposition to the plan

11. (*n.*) wickedness, sin; a grossly immoral act

    a den of _____

Group B

panegyric (pan ə 'jī rik)
pillory ('pil ə rē)
pittance ('pit əns)
presage ('pres ij)
progeny ('präj ə nē)
promulgate ('präm əl gāt)

recrimination (ri krim ə 'nā shən)
rectitude ('rek tə tüd)
restive ('res tiv)
seraphic (sə 'raf ik)
subsist (səb 'sist)

12. (*v.*) to have existence; to remain alive, manage to make a living or maintain life; persist or continue

    _____ on a diet of vegetables

13. (*n.*) descendants, offspring, children; followers, disciples

    guaranteed to us and our _____

14. (*v.*) to proclaim or issue officially; to make known far and wide

    _____ a law

15. (*adj.*) restless, hard to manage, balky

    a _____ horse

16. (*v.*) to foreshadow or point to a future event; to predict; (*n.*) a warning or indication of the future

    _____ death and destruction

17. (*n.*) a device for publicly punishing offenders; a means for exposing one to public contempt or ridicule; (*v.*) to expose to public contempt or ridicule

    _____ one's political opponents

18. (*n.*) an exchange of charges or accusations; a bitter retort or countercharge

    refrain from _____

19. (*adj.*) angelic, heavenly, celestial

    a _____ smile

20. (*n.*) a woefully meager allowance, wage, or portion

    a mere _____

21. (*n.*) formal or elaborate praise; a tribute

    a fulsome _____

22. (*n.*) uprightness, righteousness; correctness

    a person of unquestionable _____

Completing the Sentence

Choose the word for this unit that best completes each of the following sentences. Write it in the space given.

1. The wranglers began to suspect that there were wolves or mountain lions about when the herd suddenly grew nervous and _____ .

2. After a few days in which everything went my way, I suddenly learned just how _____ Lady Luck can be.

3. It was the _____ of its natural setting on those rolling hills that led the builder to dub the estate "Mount Pleasant."

4. The _____ on most cameras can be adjusted to admit more or less light, as required.

5. For many ancient peoples, the appearance of a comet was a fearful omen that _____ a great social upheaval of some kind.

6. The President has _____ a policy that commits the nation to a many-sided effort to curb the pollution of our environment.

7. Nutritionists say that most of us could _____ quite well on a great deal less food than we actually consume.

8. We hardly knew whether to laugh or cry at the silly _____ of a 17-year-old trying to act like a sophisticated man of the world.

9. Authoritarian governments often resort to violence and coercion in their efforts to repress political _____ .

10. Am I to be _____ before the entire student body because I made a few minor mistakes as a member of the Student Council?

11. The Bible tells us that visitors to the court of Solomon, the great Hebrew king, willingly did _____ unto him.

12. "I'm afraid that the child's _____ countenance belies the devilry in his heart," I observed sadly.

13. Imagine someone with my _____ tastes having to live for a week on that watery mush!

14. He inveighs against the sins of society with all the stridency of an Old Testament prophet castigating the _____ of the ungodly.

15. Though I'm by no means _____ with my money, I don't hoard it either.

16. The biography is a pretty evenhanded appraisal of the man's strengths and weaknesses, not just another _____ to a great hero.

17. We are sure that their vow is _____ because their sense of moral obligation will prevent them from ever breaking it.

18. Conscientious parents will do everything they can to foster and develop the _____ intellectual curiosity of a small child.

19. The judge's attempts to reconcile the estranged couple ended in failure when they began to hurl _____ at each other.

20. I see no reason to question the _____ of her dealings with us because I know her to be "as honest as the day is long."

21. The liberties that we have inherited from our forefathers are a sacred trust that we must hand on undiminished to our _____ .

22. Our financial standards are so different that what she considers a mere _____ seems a fortune to me.

Synonyms   *Choose the word for this unit that is most nearly **the same** in meaning as each of the following items. Write it in the space given.*

1. hedonistic, sybaritic; discriminating   _____

2. respect, deference, homage; a bow   _____

3. to augur, portend, foretell   _____

4. children, issue, posterity, offspring   _____

5. to proclaim, announce; to issue   _____

6. to last, persist; to survive; to sustain   _____

7. a modicum, trifle, "peanuts"   _____

8. prodigal, spendthrift, extravagant   _____

9. angelic, cherubic, heavenly, celestial   _____

10. a countercharge, retort   _____

11. a pose, pretense, mannerism   _____

12. disagreement, dissent, disaffection   _____

13. budding, incipient, embryonic   _____

14. an opening, gap, orifice, hole   _____

15. restless, uneasy, fidgety; recalcitrant   _____

16. a tribute, encomium, testimonial   _____

17. probity, integrity; correctness   _____

18. wickedness, evil; a crime, sin   _____

19. to expose to public abuse or ridicule   _____

20. changeable, variable, fickle   _____

21. pleasantness; social conventions   _____

22. sacred, sacrosanct, unassailable   _____

Antonyms   _Choose the word for this unit that is most nearly_ **_opposite_** _in meaning to each of the following items. Write it in the space given._

1. thrifty, frugal, economical, cautious   _____

2. a closure, blockage, occlusion   _____

3. probity, rectitude, uprightness   _____

4. changeless, steadfast, constant   _____

5. a diatribe, tirade, philippic   _____

6. ancestors, forebears, antecedents   _____

7. iniquity, heinousness, moral turpitude   _____

8. devilish, impish   _____

9. naturalness, artlessness, sincerity   _____

10. agreement, harmony, concord   _____

11. dying, moribund, senescent   _____

12. a fortune; a generous allowance   _____

13. serene, unruffled; docile   _____

14. disagreeableness, unpleasantness   _____

15. ascetic, self-denying, abstemious   _____

16. irreverence, disrespect, disregard   _____

17. vulnerable, open to attack, assailable   _____

18. to praise, extol, laud, acclaim   _____

19. to withdraw, retract; to abrogate, nullify   _____

Choosing the Right Word   _Encircle the_ **_boldface_** _word that more satisfactorily completes each of the following sentences._

1. One cannot expect a(n) (**epicurean, nascent**) democracy to go through its early years without experiencing serious growing pains.

2. Instead of hurling ugly (**recriminations, panegyrics**) at each other for the failure, let's try calmly to determine what went wrong.

3. Liberty (**subsists, presages**) only so long as people have the intelligence to know their rights and the courage to defend them.

4. Instead of being so concerned with the (**iniquities, apertures**) of others, they would do well to concentrate on correcting their own shortcomings.

5. Specific customs vary widely in different lands, but the basic (**affectations, amenities**) of civilized living are much the same everywhere.

6. Instead of mouthing empty (**panegyrics, apertures**) to the Bill of Rights, let's strive to make this great document a reality in our lives.

7. "Angelica" is indeed an apt name for one whose (**mutable, seraphic**) beauty is complemented by such sweetness of temper and gentleness of spirit.

8. Recently, the Principal (**promulgated, presaged**) a new dress code that did away with some of the unnecessary strictness of the old rules.

9. There was a loophole in the law, and through this (**aperture, obeisance**) the defendant escaped the legal consequences of his crime.

10. The study of government shows us that many political institutions thought to be unchanging are in fact highly (**inviolable, mutable**).

11. Like so many others of his generation, he did unquestioning (**iniquity, obeisance**) to the accepted symbols of material success.

12. The new "gourmet" deli features delicacies that are bound to delight even the most exacting of (**epicurean, nascent**) palates.

13. We would like to believe that the intensifying fear of ecological catastrophe (**subsists, presages**) an era of environmental harmony in the near future.

14. The novel centers on a(n) (**improvident, seraphic**) young man who squanders his inheritance on riotous living and dies in the poorhouse.

15. The resounding victory we scored at the polls is an eloquent tribute to the (**rectitude, dissidence**) of her approach as campaign manager.

16. The ability to use Standard English is not an (**aperture, affectation**) but a necessity if one is to succeed in today's business world.

17. Religious (**obeisance, dissidence**) was one of the motives that led many people to leave their homes and found colonies in North America.

18. No matter how well defended, no boundary is (**inviolable, restive**) unless the peoples on either side of it respect each other.

19. The cost of living has risen so sharply that a salary that was adequate a decade ago is now no more than a mere (**panegyric, pittance**).

20. I realize the official made a serious mistake, but that is no reason to (**pillory, subsist**) him so unmercifully in the press.

21. As the speaker's remarks became more inflammatory, the crowd grew more sullen and (**nascent, restive**).

22. Writers often regard their works as their (**dissidence, progeny**) in much the same way as other people regard their pets as family members.

Review Units 13–15

Analogies *In each of the following, choose the item that best completes the comparison.*

1. **hypnotist** is to **mesmerize** as
a. enchantress is to bewitch
b. behemoth is to bless
c. nostrum is to injure
d. canard is to attract

2. **bon vivant** is to **epicurean** as
a. lazybones is to febrile
b. merchant is to abstruse
c. spoilsport is to decorous
d. ascetic is to austere

3. **improvident** is to **foresight** as
a. immense is to size
b. impartial is to bias
c. impassive is to sense
d. immune is to protection

4. **mutable** is to **change** as
a. cognizant is to decay
b. durable is to wear
c. mortal is to death
d. divine is to aging

5. **pillory** is to **punish** as
a. gallows is to trap
b. rack is to torture
c. derrick is to kill
d. scaffold is to reform

6. **progeny** is to **after** as
a. ancestors are to before
b. contemporaries are to after
c. relatives are to before
d. antecedents are to after

7. **cynosure** is to **magnet** as
a. moratorium is to spark plug
b. euphemism is to fuse
c. coup is to safety valve
d. firebrand is to catalyst

8. **contrite** is to **remorse** as
a. crestfallen is to delight
b. morose is to pleasure
c. jubilant is to joy
d. pensive is to elation

9. **ghoul** is to **graves** as
a. shoplifter is to stores
b. cat burglar is to animals
c. corsair is to planes
d. poacher is to eggs

10. **ethereal** is to **heaven** as
a. visionary is to purgatory
b. cosmic is to moon
c. infernal is to hell
d. seraphic is to earth

11. **beatific** is to **bliss** as
a. loath is to repose
b. serene is to calm
c. febrile is to ease
d. nascent is to tranquillity

12. **desiccated** is to **moisture** as
a. arid is to warmth
b. replete is to plenitude
c. dexterous is to agility
d. wizened is to smoothness

13. **facade** is to **building** as
a. cover is to book
b. lid is to jar
c. window is to door
d. eraser is to pencil

14. **pittance** is to **quantity** as
a. trickle is to range
b. smidgen is to quality
c. handful is to number
d. iota is to scope

15. **cacophony** is to **hear** as
a. opprobrium is to taste
b. dissidence is to smell
c. hubbub is to feel
d. chaos is to see

16. **seraphic** is to **angel** as
a. impish is to cherub
b. diabolic is to devil
c. monstrous is to spirit
d. ghoulish is to pariah

17. **cajole** is to **blandishments** as
a. intimidate is to threats
b. coerce is to accolades
c. flatter is to rebukes
d. affront is to compliments

18. **restive** is to **control** as
a. tractable is to lead
b. docile is to manage
c. insubordinate is to obey
d. elusive is to grasp

19. portent is to **presage** as
a. aperture is to preempt
b. signal is to indicate
c. flare is to engender
d. obeisance is to warn

20. manifest is to **see** as
a. audible is to listen
b. mobile is to lift
c. tangible is to touch
d. edible is to enjoy

Identification   In each of the following groups, encircle the word that is best defined or suggested by the introductory phrase.

1. "underprivileged" instead of "poor"
a. imminent   b. euphemism   c. promulgate   d. febrile

2. "I rise to dispute the accuracy of the statements made by the last speaker."
a. gainsay   b. loath   c. complaisant   d. desiccated

3. a remark made deliberately to cause offense
a. deign   b. contrite   c. seraphic   d. affront

4. an air-conditioned room with color TV and private bath
a. amenities   b. facades   c. efficacies   d. pittance

5. pulled some strings to get a contract
a. pillory   b. panegyric   c. chicanery   d. improvident

6. an unpopular student avoided by everyone
a. pariah   b. deign   c. progeny   d. dissidence

7. an attitude of respect and awe upon meeting a world-famous writer
a. loath   b. recrimination   c. obeisance   d. coup

8. the first faint stirrings of an idea
a. iniquity   b. nascent   c. wizened   d. ethereal

9. obvious enough to be readily perceived by all
a. manifest   b. incongruous   c. aperture   d. beatific

10. unshakable moral integrity
a. replete   b. rectitude   c. restive   d. opprobrium

11. relies on chicken soup as a remedy for all disorders of body and mind
a. nostrum   b. aperture   c. coup   d. mutable

12. a brilliant oratorical style that left the audience spellbound
a. engender   b. mesmerize   c. subsist   d. simplistic

13. "That weird story about me has absolutely no basis in fact."
a. replete   b. abstruse   c. canard   d. complaisant

14. someone who is the center of attention
a. machination   b. cynosure   c. presage   d. cacophonous

15. "Flattery will get you nowhere!"
a. putative   b. preempt   c. affectation   d. blandishments

16. a charming young person who behaves with outstanding propriety
a. cognizant   b. decorous   c. epicurean   d. mutable

17. a battleship next to a rowboat
a. manifest   b. restive   c. subsist   d. behemoth

18. barely enough to make ends meet
   a. canard   b. pittance   c. amenity   d. coup

19. how you might characterize an instinct
   a. facade   b. ghoulish   c. innate   d. captious

20. shipped the equipment to the buyer by parcel post
   a. consign   b. moratorium   c. minutiae   d. putative

Shades of Meaning   *Read each sentence carefully. Then encircle the item that best completes the statement below the sentence.*

Ralph Waldo Emerson, the Sage of Concord and the guiding light of American transcendentalism, counted among his progeny such distinguished contemporaries as Henry Thoreau, Margaret Fuller, and Orestes Brownson.

(2)

(4)

1. The word **progeny** in line 2 is used to mean
   a. children   c. offspring
   b. disciples   d. descendants

In *The Autocrat of the Breakfast-Table* Oliver Wendell Holmes paraphrases Plutarch's "Epicurean paradox" this way: "Give us the luxuries of life, and we will dispense with its necessaries."

(2)

2. The best definition for the word **Epicurean** in line 2 is
   a. pursuing pleasure   c. insoluble
   b. discriminating   d. ancient

Only a historian of great imaginative power could extract from the desiccated figures of dusty old ledger books the drama of a great family's decline.

(2)

3. In line 2 the word **desiccated** most nearly means
   a. complicated   c. thoroughly dried out
   b. shriveled   d. arid and uninteresting

The proposed bill sparked controversy from the moment it was introduced. There was even a tug-of-war between chairpersons over which congressional committee was properly cognizant.

(2)

4. The word **cognizant** in line 3 is used to mean
   a. knowledgeable   c. having jurisdiction
   b. informed   d. aware

"But would the honest patriot, in the full tide of successful experiment, abandon a government which has so far kept us free and firm, on the theoretic and visionary fear that this government, the world's best hope, may by possibility want energy to preserve itself?"
          (Thomas Jefferson, "First Inaugural Address")

(2)

(4)

5. In line 3 the word **visionary** is best defined as
   a. utopian   c. idealistic
   b. fantastic   d. predictable

R

Antonyms   *In each of the following groups, encircle the word or expression that is most nearly **opposite** in meaning to the word in **boldface type** in the introductory phrase.*

1. growing **dissidence** in the party
a. agreement   b. opposition   c. debt   d. intrigue

2. a **complaisant** employee
a. sophisticated   b. uncooperative   c. quiet   d. diligent

3. **epicurean** tastes
a. hedonistic   b. ascetic   c. refined   d. predictable

4. **abstruse** language
a. poetic   b. foreign   c. straightforward   d. fallacious

5. an **imminent** thunderstorm
a. looming   b. distant   c. sudden   d. destructive

6. **inviolable** principles
a. honest   b. fundamental   c. vulnerable   d. sound

7. seemed **loath** to enter
a. unwilling   b. eager   c. afraid   d. unable

8. **promulgate** a policy
a. enforce   b. formulate   c. issue   d. withdraw

9. a **contrite** lawbreaker
a. apologetic   b. unrepentant   c. repeat   d. accused

10. an **improvident** manager
a. incompetent   b. inexperienced   c. shortsighted   d. cautious

11. **engender** misunderstandings
a. deter   b. beget   c. aggravate   d. exploit

12. **cognizant of** all the facts
a. informed of   b. guided by   c. unaware of   d. requiring

13. **pilloried** in the marketplace
a. ridiculed   b. caricatured   c. censored   d. extolled

14. a lengthy **panegyric**
a. obituary   b. tribute   c. introduction   d. denunciation

15. an **ethereal** vision
a. infernal   b. heavenly   c. abnormal   d. illusory

16. a **cacophonous** piece of music
a. modern   b. harmonious   c. dissonant   d. classical

17. a **desiccated** landscape
a. parched   b. polluted   c. sodden   d. hardened

18. a **captious** remark
a. irrelevant   b. malicious   c. uncritical   d. brilliant

19. an **incongruous** combination
a. complex   b. compatible   c. jarring   d. vivid

20. the **iniquity** of the act
a. daring   b. wickedness   c. rectitude   d. skill

Completing the Sentence

From the following lists of words, choose the one that best completes each of the sentences below. Write the word in the appropriate space.

Group A

decorous	blandishment	preempt	imminent
deign	amenity	captious	putative
minutiae	recrimination	engender	ethereal

1. The _____ benefits of the new drug must be weighed against the possible disadvantages of its use before it can be approved.
2. The whole purpose of this campaign is neither to support nor to oppose the program but simply to _____ more public interest in the issues involved.
3. Because of their relatively low price, paperback books have been able to _____ a large part of the market once dominated by hardbound books.
4. Now that you have been chosen the "student most likely to succeed," will you _____ to recognize your old friends?
5. Instead of exchanging bitter _____ about the causes of the fiasco, let's put our heads together and try to repair the damage.
6. The lawyers became so entangled in the _____ of the case that they lost sight of the overriding legal principles at issue.

Group B

moratorium	consign	ghoulish	restive
machination	promulgate	coup	aperture
pillory	contrite	presage	subsist

1. As soon as this brilliant actress appeared on the stage, the crowd that had been so _____ settled down and gave its full attention to the performance.
2. Is this fine public servant to be _____ in the press simply because he made an honest mistake of judgment?
3. Hikers lost in the wilderness have been known to _____ for weeks on roots and berries.
4. Since they persist in their senseless opposition to the plan, we hereby _____ them to the deepest regions of the netherworld.
5. The university imposed a(n) _____ on athletic scholarships until charges lodged against its sports program were fully investigated.

6. The fact that you are duly _____ about your inexcusable blunder does nothing to repair the damage you have caused.

7. Horror writers like Stephen King seem to take a(n) _____ delight in the gruesome scenes they depict so vividly.

Word Families

A. *On the line provided, write a **noun form** of each of the following words.*

EXAMPLE: manifest—**manifestation**

1. cacophonous _____

2. consign _____

3. imminent _____

4. cognizant _____

5. decorous _____

6. improvident _____

7. complaisant _____

8. ghoulish _____

9. incongruous _____

10. desiccated _____

11. subsist _____

12. mesmerize _____

13. promulgate _____

14. contrite _____

15. mutable _____

B. *On the line provided, write a **verb** related to each of the following words.*

EXAMPLE: dissidence—**dissent**

1. visionary _____

2. mutable _____

3. recrimination _____

4. machination _____

5. inviolable _____

6. desiccated _____

7. blandishment _____

8. improvident _____

9. cognizant _____

10. wizened _____

C. *On the line provided, write an* **adjective** *related to each of the following words.*

EXAMPLE: efficacy—**efficacious**

1. opprobrium _____

2. preempt _____

3. euphemism _____

4. dissidence _____

5. iniquity _____

6. recrimination _____

Filling the Blanks — *Encircle the pair of expressions that best complete the meaning of each of the following passages.*

1. Disgruntled army officers and other _____ elements in the society engineered the bloody _____ that toppled the duly elected government a few months after it had taken office.

   a. contrite . . . nostrum   c. visionary . . .pittance
   b. restive . . . moratorium   d. dissident . . . coup

2. Behind the courtier's outward _____ of decorous sloth there lurked the _____ imagination of an inveterate opportunist, eager to capitalize on any windfall that came his way.

   a. aperture . . . incongruous   c. cynosure . . . nascent
   b. facade . . . febrile   d. affectation . . . improvident

3. Any official who is genuinely concerned about the _____ of his or her behavior while in public office will think twice before engaging in the kinds of political _____ and back-room shenanigans that sometimes go on when a juicy government contract is up for grabs.

   a. rectitude . . . chicanery   c. progeny . . . machinations
   b. imminence . . . blandishments   d. iniquity . . . cognizance

4. Once the news broke, the public heaped so much _____ on the head of the hapless city official that he soon found himself a veritable political _____ , even in his own party.

   a. euphemism . . . canard   c. opprobrium . . . pariah
   b. affectation . . . amenity   d. efficacy . . . ghoul

5. As soon as the famous movie star walked into my shop, she became the _____ of all eyes. Customers stopped what they were doing to stare at her as if _____ by the spell of her celebrity.

   a. aperture . . . engendered   c. moratorium . . . preempted
   b. cynosure . . . mesmerized   d. pillory . . . promulgated

Analogies   *In each of the following, encircle the item that best completes the comparison.*

1. encomium is to **panegyric** as
a. diatribe is to harangue
b. facade is to cynosure
c. canard is to verity
d. eulogy is to philippic

2. amenity is to **asperity** as
a. complicity is to collusion
b. rectitude is to iniquity
c. affectation is to euphemism
d. moratorium is to hiatus

3. myopic is to **discernment** as
a. pertinacious is to determination
b. imperturbable is to composure
c. improvident is to foresight
d. cognizant is to awareness

4. misanthrope is to **gregarious** as
a. pickpocket is to furtive
b. liar is to mendacious
c. lackey is to obsequious
d. hero is to pusillanimous

5. loath is to **reluctance** as
a. insatiable is to boredom
b. blasé is to concern
c. avid is to enthusiasm
d. fervent is to apathy

6. pariah is to **opprobrium** as
a. aesthete is to ignominy
b. celebrity is to acclamation
c. victor is to recrimination
d. saint is to malediction

7. penitent is to **contrite** as
a. unwonted is to intractable
b. sumptuous is to depraved
c. visionary is to utopian
d. pecuniary is to cacophonous

8. desiccate is to **heat** as
a. saturate is to liquid
b. mesmerize is to air
c. rebuff is to wax
d. burnish is to fire

9. captious is to **cavil** as
a. disgruntled is to grouse
b. complaisant is to demur
c. febrile is to importune
d. chary is to allege

10. stratagem is to **crafty** as
a. chicanery is to overt
b. peregrination is to coherent
c. juggernaut is to picayune
d. machination is to devious

Shades of Meaning   *Read each sentence carefully. Then encircle the item that best completes the statement below the sentence.*

"All the choir of heaven and furniture of earth . . . have not subsistence without a mind."   (Bishop Berkeley, *Principles of Human Knowledge*)   (2)

1. In line 1 the word **subsistence** most nearly means
a. persistence   b. sustenance   c. existence   d. continuance

Even a lubber like myself could see by the quickening breeze and the swell of the sea that a mighty blow was engendering to windward.   (2)

2. The word **engendering** in line 2 is used to mean
a. forming   b. producing   c. causing   d. subsiding

Archaeologists could only wonder that objects so ethereal had survived intact the rude treatment of the grave robbers.   (2)

3. The best definition for the word **ethereal** in line 1 is
a. heavenly   b. airy   c. celestial   d. delicate

Of all the celestial bodies that crowd the night sky none is a more faithful and steadfast cynosure to the navigator than the North Star.   (2)

4. In line 2 the word **cynosure** is used to mean
- a. center of attraction
- b. guiding light
- c. object of beauty
- d. focal point

"The sumptuous feast the careworn king consumes,
Though served on gold or plate or china fine,   **(2)**
Ofttimes tastes not so wholesome or so sweet
As lowly cotter's porridge, set out plain   **(4)**
In sylvan trencher carved by his own hand
Of mighty oak or aspen quaking or tall pine."   **(6)**
    (A.E. Glug, "Runes," 6–11)

5. The word **sylvan** in line 5 most nearly means
- a. made of wood
- b. pertaining to woods
- c. living in the forest
- d. mythical

**Filling
the Blanks**
*Encircle the pair of words that best complete the
meaning of each of the following passages.*

1. As soon as they received the appropriate order from the court, the local
cemetery workers began the somewhat _____ business of
_____ the victim's body and delivering it to the coroner for
reexamination.
- a. nefarious . . . interpolating
- b. macabre . . . excoriating
- c. abject . . . promulgating
- d. ghoulish . . . exhuming

2. If the government's approach to complicated international problems is too
_____ , it runs the risk of _____ rather than
solving them.
- a. simplistic . . . exacerbating
- b. prestigious . . . emending
- c. tenable . . . propounding
- d. peremptory . . . requiting

3. "A century ago it may have been possible to _____ on
pennies a day," I replied firmly to the personnel manager, "but I don't
see how you can really expect a person to live on the mere
_____ you are proposing to pay me."
- a. calumniate . . . nostrum
- b. accost . . . talisman
- c. subsist . . . pittance
- d. deign . . . figment

4. A _____ should stick to the _____ of a sport
and leave its finer points to the experts.
- a. pedant . . . exigencies
- b. neophyte . . . rudiments
- c. dilettante . . . idiosyncrasies
- d. tyro . . . minutiae

5. The rather straitlaced Victorians, who were overly concerned about the
_____ of a person's behavior, would certainly have looked
_____ at the casualness of modern social conventions.
- a. propinquity . . . summarily
- b. celerity . . . reputedly
- c. propriety . . . askance
- d. sophistry . . . indubitably

Final Mastery Test

I. Selecting Word Meanings

*In each of the following groups, encircle the word or expression that is most nearly **the same** in meaning as the word in **boldface type** in the introductory phrase.*

1. **substantiate** a statement
   a. reveal   b. verify   c. deny   d. amplify

2. drew water from a **brackish** stream
   a. muddy   b. salty   c. fast-moving   d. quiet

3. **avid** advocates of democracy
   a. cynical   b. lukewarm   c. enthusiastic   d. famous

4. disappointed by their **myopic** outlook
   a. nasty   b. insincere   c. pessimistic   d. shortsighted

5. resented their **mordant** remarks
   a. sarcastic   b. offhand   c. profane   d. irrelevant

6. cleared up the **discrepancy**
   a. motive   b. negligence   c. inconsistency   d. mess

7. the **flotsam** of a big city
   a. skyscrapers   b. pollution   c. vagrants   d. exploiters

8. composed the **eulogy**
   a. critique   b. tribute   c. concerto   d. satire

9. rule by **fiat**
   a. consent   b. democracy   c. whim   d. decree

10. an **abject** beggar
    a. carefree   b. fearless   c. wretched   d. wandering

11. the only member to **demur**
    a. accept   b. volunteer   c. object   d. applaud

12. had the **effrontery** to laugh
    a. desire   b. gall   c. sense   d. humor

13. their **picayune** criticisms
    a. trifling   b. humorous   c. irrelevant   d. vicious

14. **portend** a life-or-death struggle
    a. overcome   b. prevent   c. foreshadow   d. decide

15. the **mandate** of the people
    a. betrayal   b. objection   c. folly   d. authorization

16. yielded **paltry** results
    a. overwhelming   b. insignificant   c. ruinous   d. beneficial

17. **deprecate** such behavior
    a. approve   b. deplore   c. analyze   d. improve

18. the **asperities** of life
    a. rewards   b. severities   c. uncertainties   d. pastimes

19. saw **substantive** improvements
    a. minor   b. final   c. major   d. needed

20. **raze** the tenements
    a. renovate   b. appraise   c. demolish   d. condemn

21. the **nadir** of my fortunes
    a. twist   b. bottom   c. irony   d. pinnacle

22. **cognizant of** the facts
    a. informed of   b. ignorant of   c. indifferent to   d. indignant about

23. **deign** to acknowledge my presence
    a. seem   b. stoop   c. refuse   d. attempt

24. a **moratorium** on the sale of arms
    a. emphasis   b. suspension   c. penalty   d. symposium

25. delivered a **panegyric**
    a. explanation   b. rebuke   c. apology   d. encomium

II. Word Pairs   *In the space before each of the following pairs of words write:*

        S — if the words are synonyms or near-synonyms.
        O — if the words are antonyms or near-antonyms.
        N — if the words are not directly related in meaning.

_____ **26.** moot — indisputable   _____ **34.** preempt — fatuous

_____ **27.** arrogate — renounce   _____ **35.** laconic — terse

_____ **28.** saturnine — morose   _____ **36.** shortcoming — foible

_____ **29.** detritus — gambit   _____ **37.** moribund — thriving

_____ **30.** derogatory — pejorative   _____ **38.** ubiquitous — omnipresent

_____ **31.** flatter — calumniate   _____ **39.** chicanery — flaccid

_____ **32.** frenetic — calm   _____ **40.** feckless — effective

_____ **33.** relentless — inexorable

III. Words That Describe People   *In the space before each word in Column A, write the **letter** of the corresponding brief description in Column B.*

Column A	Column B
_____ **41. derelict**	a. one who hates all people
_____ **42. tyro**	b. a person given to impractical schemes
_____ **43. incumbent**	c. an extremely patriotic person
_____ **44. charlatan**	d. a rank beginner
_____ **45. penitent**	e. a faker
_____ **46. agnostic**	f. a sorcerer
_____ **47. visionary**	g. one who implores
_____ **48. suppliant**	h. a current officeholder
_____ **49. misanthrope**	i. a homeless wanderer
_____ **50. necromancer**	j. a religious skeptic
	k. one who regrets misdeeds

FMT

IV. Words That Describe Physical Qualities

*Some words that describe physical qualities are listed in Column A. Next to each item, write the **letter** of the corresponding brief description in Column B.*

Column A	Column B
_____ 51. viscous	a. dried out
_____ 52. piquant	b. unpleasant to the ear
_____ 53. desiccated	c. a delicate gradation
_____ 54. murky	d. shining brightly
_____ 55. refulgent	e. to raise to a greater height
_____ 56. cacophonous	f. lacking clarity
_____ 57. oscillate	g. thick and gluey
_____ 58. propinquity	h. having a sharp, savory taste
_____ 59. congeal	i. blocking out light
_____ 60. nuance	j. nearness
	k. to swing back and forth
	l. to thicken or coagulate

V. Words of Evaluation

Some words that indicate favorable or unfavorable evaluations are listed below. They may apply to people, things, language, etc. Write the appropriate word on the line next to each of the following descriptive sentences.

Group A

simplistic	ethereal	overweening	pedantry
dilettante	garish	sylvan	sacrilege
decorous	carping	felicitous	ebullient
banal	perspicacity	profane	pariah

61. The plot of the soap opera was so familiar, stale, and predictable that we soon stopped watching it. _____

62. Her poetry seems to carry beyond the gross substance of this world into the realm of pure spirit. _____

63. She is terribly overdressed—too many jewels, too many bright colors, too many fancy frills. _____

64. He keeps bringing literary allusions into his conversation even though he knows most people won't understand them. _____

65. Her unfailingly lively and high-spirited personality makes her delightful company. _____

66. He has considerable talent as a painter, but since he is unwilling to work at that profession seriously, he will never accomplish much. _____

67. Don't you realize that you will discourage and antagonize people by that constant, petty criticism? _____

68. Even in casual conversation, his language seems to provide exactly the right word for any purpose or situation. _____

69. Because he has an exaggerated idea of his own importance, he assumes an arrogant attitude in dealing with other people. _____

70. She is a brilliant executive because she sees through surface appearances and gets right down to the heart of a problem. _____

Group B

lackadaisical	**bestial**	**benign**	**pusillanimous**
redolent	**incendiary**	**sophistry**	**prepossessing**
pertinacious	**mundane**	**inane**	**mendacious**
prestigious	**incongruous**	**mutable**	**ephemeral**

71. Their behavior was so devoid of all moral standards that it seemed subhuman. _____

72. Once Tom begins something, he sticks to it until it's completed. _____

73. The arguments presented in the editorial look good at first, but they are full of deceptive half-truths and clever fallacies. _____

74. In their efforts to be amusing, they succeed only in being silly and vapid. _____

75. Their policy of "peace at any price" was denounced by the opposition as craven appeasement. _____

76. His greatest weakness is that he does everything in a half-hearted way, without drive or enthusiasm. _____

77. That university is renowned as a leading center of research and scholarship. _____

78. Telling lies is not just an occasional thing with him but a way of life. _____

79. His remarks seemed calculated to ignite the heated feelings of his audience. _____

80. Don't you think that a high-rise office tower would look out of place in that residential neighborhood? _____

VI. Word Associations

*In each of the following, encircle the expression that best completes the meaning of the sentence, with particular reference to the meaning of the word in **boldface type**.*

81. If you **temporize** when a decision is called for, you are
a. acting decisively
b. stalling for time
c. misjudging the situation
d. losing your temper

82. A taxi driver who takes you to your destination by a **devious** route may be
a. trying to build up the fare
b. getting rid of you quickly
c. showing off his driving skill
d. saving you money

83. You would be well advised not to give **credence** to
a. your friends
b. your creditors
c. a reliable witness
d. a habitual liar

84. Which advice would be most suitable for a person who is **recumbent**?
a. "Keep your eye on the ball."
b. "Rise and shine!"
c. "Turn left at the first light."
d. "Grin and bear it."

85. A **figment** usually develops in
a. a factory
b. an orchard
c. the human mind
d. the wild blue yonder

86. The wisest course of action when confronted by a **juggernaut** is to
a. get out of its way
b. take its picture
c. stand your ground
d. make up your mind

87. A **melange** always contains
a. vegetables but not meat
b. costly French sauces
c. kosher food
d. diverse bits and pieces

88. In a **convivial** atmosphere, people may be expected to
a. suffer from boredom
b. enjoy themselves
c. go into shock
d. show off their erudition

89. one's **progeny** might include
a. trophies and awards
b. fame and fortune
c. sons and daughters
d. assets and liabilities

90. Which of the following can be **abrogated**?
a. mother and child
b. tonsils and adenoids
c. the ups and downs of life
d. contracts and treaties

91. Typical **amenities** of urban life might include
a. air pollution and litter
b. muggings on the street
c. traffic jams
d. museums and concerts

92. To **allege** that someone is guilty of a crime means that
a. the person is clearly guilty
b. the charge remains to be proved
c. the charge is malicious
d. an indictment will be handed down

93. **Wraiths** abound in
a. department stores
b. vacation spots
c. ghost stories
d. TV commercials

94. If your interests are **ramified,** they are
a. in many different fields
b. concerned with trees
c. intellectual
d. too vague to describe

95. The **motif** of a play refers to its
a. financial backing
b. adaptation for television
c. basic theme
d. cast of characters

96. Which would be a **coup** for a diplomat?
a. arranging an advantageous treaty
b. being sent home
c. taking a vacation
d. retiring after 40 years of service

97. A remark you might expect to hear from someone who is **impecunious** is
a. "Let me pay for it."
b. "Keep the change."
c. "Can you change a fifty?"
d. "Why am I always broke?"

98. Histrionic behavior is best suited to
a. the stage
b. the laboratory
c. the classroom
d. the museum

99. An example of a **euphemism** is
a. "old man" for "father"
b. "boob tube" for "television"
c. "liberate" for "steal"
d. "indeterminate" for "unsettled"

100. Plaintive tones may issue from you if you
a. get a good night's sleep
b. receive a compliment
c. do well on this Final Test
d. do poorly on this Final Test

Units 1–3

cred—to believe

This root appears in **credence** (page 19), which means "belief or mental acceptance." Some other words based on the same root are listed below.

accreditation	**credibility**	**creditor**	**credulity**
credentials	**creditable**	**credo**	**credulous**

From the list of words above, choose the one that corresponds to each of the brief definitions below. Write the word on the line at the right of the definition and in the illustrative phrase below it.

1. references, testimonials, or other (usually written) evidence of identity or status (*"that which provides a basis for belief"*) _____

demand to see their _____

2. inclined to believe very readily, gullible _____

as _____ as a child

3. believability _____

questioned the _____ of the advertisement

4. a statement or summary of faith or fundamental belief; an authoritative statement of religious belief (*"I believe"*) _____

a scientist's _____

5. bringing or deserving credit or honor _____

did a(n) _____ job

6. an undue readiness to believe; a lack of critical judgment _____

exploited their _____

7. official authorization or approval (often used in regard to academic affairs) _____

a new university seeking _____

8. a person or an organization to which money is owed _____

dunned by one's _____

From the list of words above, choose the one that best completes each of the following sentences. Write the word in the space provided.

1. In view of the number of weeks he had been absent from class, he gave a very

_____ performance on the math final.

2. The salesman who made all those absurd claims about the used car was trying to take advantage of our _____ .

3. The new medical school will start to accept students and organize classes as soon as it receives its official _____ .

4. A physician's _____ is aptly summarized in the noble ideas and attitudes set forth in the Hippocratic oath.

5. As soon as the new ambassador arrived, he called on the foreign minister and presented his _____ .

6. A series of financial setbacks plunged him into debt, and he was reduced to dodging his relentless _____ .

7. The plot turned on a series of coincidences so farfetched as to tax the patience of even the most _____ of readers.

8. The lawyer tried to attack Mr. Summer's _____ as a witness by showing that he had a poor reputation for honesty and reliability.

Units 4–6

ject—thrown, to throw

This root appears in **abject** (page 43), which means "miserable, wretched, degraded, or hopeless" (literally, "thrown down"). Some other words and expressions based on the same root are listed below.

dejection	**objectivity**	**objet d'art**	**subjective**
interject	**object lesson**	**projectile**	**trajectory**

From the list of words above, choose the one that corresponds to each of the brief definitions below. Write the word on the line at the right of the definition and in the illustrative phrase below it.

1. an article of artistic value _____

a collector of Oriental _____

2. the ability to see things as they really are, without personal prejudices or feelings; fairmindedness _____

the _____ of a scientist

3. the path of a moving body or object _____

the _____ of a rocket

4. an object that can be thrown, hurled, or shot, such as a spear or bullet (*"that which is thrown ahead"*) _____

the sharp point of the _____

5. to insert, throw in, or introduce between other things (*"to throw between"*)

_____ a comment _____

6. an incident or reference that teaches a principle through a concrete illustration or practical example

a painful _____ _____

7. the state of being depressed or low in spirit, despondency, sadness

a mood of profound _____ _____

8. existing in the mind (rather than in the outer world); determined by one's personal feelings or standards

a(n) _____ reaction _____

From the list of words on page 144, choose the one that best completes each of the following sentences. Write the word in the space provided.

1. He did much to relieve the tension when he _____ that humorous anecdote into the solemn and dreary proceedings.

2. I was ready to throw out those odds and ends inherited from my grandmother, but they proved to be valuable _____ .

3. Her mood of _____ is so deep and has lasted so long that we believe she should have professional help.

4. By tracing the bullet's _____ , ballistics experts were able to pinpoint the location from which it was fired.

5. Unless you are able to view this problem with complete _____ , you are going to make decisions that will do more harm than good, however well-intended they may be.

6. I sincerely hope that losing your job because of repeated lateness will serve as an apt, if somewhat painful, _____ for you.

7. My standards of beauty are not based on any formal study or rules; they are entirely _____ .

8. For a long time, the defenders of the beseiged city kept enemy troops at bay by hurling spears, rocks, and other _____ at them from the walls.

Units 7–9

clam, claim—to cry out, shout, call

This root appears in **acclamation** (page 69). The literal meaning of acclamation is "shouting at," but it now suggests "applause" or "an overwhelmingly favorable oral vote." Some other words based on the same root are listed below.

acclaim	**clamorous**	**disclaimer**	**proclamation**
claimant	**declaim**	**irreclaimable**	**reclamation**

From the list of words above, choose the one that corresponds to each of the brief definitions below. Write the word on the line at the right of the definition and in the illustrative phrase below it.

1. to speak like an orator; to recite in public, make a public speech; to speak bitterly against   _____

    _____ lines from the play

2. an official or formal public announcement   _____

    posted the _____

3. a denial or disavowal of responsibility or connection; a formal refusal of one's rights or claims   _____

    issued a(n) _____

4. incapable of being reformed; incapable of being rendered useful   _____

    _____ swampland

5. the act of bringing back or restoring to a normal or useful condition (*"to call back"*)   _____

    the _____ of the desert

6. to applaud; to indicate strong approval; noisy and enthusiastic applause   _____

    public _____

7. a person who asserts a right or title   _____

    a(n) _____ to the estate

8. marked by loud confusion or outcry; noisily insistent (*"crying out"*)   _____

    the _____ demands for reform

From the list of words above, choose the one that best completes each of the following sentences. Write the word in the space provided.

1. "By spurning every opportunity to turn from a life of crime," the judge said, "you

have proven yourself _____ ."

BWR

2. Is there anything in literature to match the eloquence of the funeral speech that

Shakespeare has Mark Anthony _____ over the body of Caesar!

3. In towns and villages throughout the realm, the king's subjects gathered to hear the

_____ announcing the birth of an heir to the throne.

4. For legal purposes, the motion picture carried a(n) _____ stating
that any resemblance between the characters portrayed and real persons was
purely coincidental.

5. The first objective of our penal system should be the _____ of the
great majority of the inmates, so that they will have a chance to lead productive
lives.

6. Though some people denounced the man as a fraud, others _____
him as a saint.

7. Although he was a(n) _____ to the throne of France, he lived for
many years as an exile, in poverty and obscurity.

8. If you are going to do a good job as a baby-sitter, you must remember not to yield

to the _____ demands of spoiled children.

Units 10–12

rog—to ask, beg, call

This root appears in **abrogate** (page 89), meaning "to cancel,
to abolish by authoritative action." Some other words based on
the same root are listed below.

abrogation	**derogation**	**interrogative**	**supererogatory**
arrogance	**interrogation**	**prorogue**	**surrogate**

---

*From the list of words above, choose the one that corresponds
to each of the brief definitions below. Write the word on the
line at the right of the definition and in the illustrative phrase
below it.*

1. exaggerated self-importance, haughty pride   _____

the _____ of power

2. an act or expression that detracts from reputation, value,
power, etc. *("to call down")*   _____

resented their _____ of my motives

3. a substitute, deputy; a judge in charge of probate of
wills, administration of estates, and appointment of
guardians; substitute   _____

served as _____ parents

4. an act of formal or systematic questioning   _____

     a police _____

5. a cancellation; the act of repealing or annulling ("*calling off*")   _____

     _____ of the agreement

6. to discontinue a session of a legislative body; to defer, postpone   _____

     _____ the assembly

7. asking a question; having the form or character of a question; a word or sentence that asks a question   _____

     the _____ form of the verb

8. performed or observed beyond the degree required, demanded, or expected; unnecessary   _____

     _____ comments

From the list of words on page 147, choose the one that best completes each of the following sentences. Write the word in the space provided.

1. The suspect was led into the _____ room, where two detectives questioned him until the wee hours of the morning.

2. It was nice of you to help Paul wash his car, but doing a complete wax job for him to boot was clearly _____ .

3. His colossal _____ led him to dismiss the feelings and concerns of his "inferiors" as scarcely worth noticing.

4. I have always found it hard to understand why "do-gooder" is used as a term of _____ , although it seems to refer to something highly admirable.

5. Since both the parents are deceased, it is up to the _____ court to see that the interests of the minor children are protected.

6. Though her comment about cleaning the room was _____ in form, it was clear that she was issuing an order, not asking a question.

7. There is no doubt that our society needs improvement, but the answer does not lie in _____ of the ideals, rules, and institutions we have inherited from the past.

8. The kings of England would often abruptly _____ Parliament to prevent passage of measures unwelcome to the throne.

Units 13–15

vid, vis—to look, see

This root appears in **visionary** (page 117), which means "lacking in practicality" or, as a noun, "a dreamer or seer." Some other words based on the same root are listed below.

advisement	**providence**	**proviso**	**visitation**
envisage	**provident**	**visage**	**vista**

From the list of words above, choose the one that corresponds to each of the brief definitions below. Write the word on the line at the right of the definition and in the illustrative phrase below it.

1. a face, countenance, appearance, look, aspect (*"that which is seen"*) _____

his _____ scarred by tragedy

2. divine guidance or care; a manifestation of such guidance _____

trusted in _____

3. a distant view or prospect through an opening; an extensive mental view _____

a breathtaking _____

4. a conditional stipulation; an article or clause in a contract that introduces a condition (*"that which is foreseen"*) _____

with the _____ that we supervise the exchange

5. a severe punishment or affliction; a visit for the purpose of making an official inspection; an act of visiting _____

a(n) _____ of the plague

6. to picture to oneself (*"see into"*) _____

_____ an America made up entirely of small farmers

7. providing for future needs or contingencies; thrifty, economical _____

a(n) _____ use of our resources

8. a careful consideration (*"act of seeing to"*) _____

take the request under _____

From the list of words above, choose the one that best completes each of the following sentences. Write the word in the space provided.

1. From the summit of the mountain, a vast _____ of lush pastures and rolling hills spread out in every direction as far as the eye could see.

2. An old maxim has it that luck is a nickname for _____ .

3. Is it possible for us to _____ a world in which there is no war, poverty, pollution, or hatred?

4. I agreed to serve as the chairperson of this year's prom committee only with the _____ that six other class members act as my assistants.

5. The scholarship committee has my application under _____ and has promised me a decision shortly.

6. It was only after I saw his gaunt eyes and haggard _____ that I began to realize just how much of an ordeal he had been through.

7. That old mansion is reputedly inhabited by some fiendish spirit, whose nocturnal _____ have frightened away anyone who has tried to live in the place.

8. If you were a little more _____ with your allowance, you wouldn't constantly need to borrow money from others.

Enhancing Your Vocabulary

Units 1–3

Expressions from Sports and Games

Since athletics plays so important a role in our daily lives, it is only natural that many colorful expressions used to describe sports and games have "spilled over" into the everyday language. One such word, **gambit,** derived from chess, was introduced on page 13. A few other examples of this phenomenon are listed below. All of them would make good additions to your active vocabulary.

front-runner
have an ace up one's sleeve
kick off
long shot
Monday-morning quarterback
par for the course

pinch-hit
put on a full-court press
showboating
start out with two strikes against you
stymied
throw in the towel

From the list of words and phrases above, choose the item that corresponds to each of the brief definitions below. Write it in the space at the right of the definition.

1. to serve as a substitute; to take over a position of responsibility in an emergency

    Source: baseball   _____

2. to attempt to overcome an opponent by contesting him or her at every opportunity, even at points where he or she might ordinarily expect to be secure

    Source: basketball   _____

3. exactly what is or was to be expected according to the accepted standard, common sense, or previous experience. (This expression is often ironically negative.)

    Source: golf   _____

4. to have an effective resource or factor held in reserve for use at a strategic point

    Source: card playing   _____

5. blocked, frustrated, or thwarted

    Source: golf   _____

6. the leader in a race or competition, especially if it is political

    Source: track   _____

7. seeking to attract attention or applause or otherwise impress people by acting in an ostentatious manner, grandstanding

    Source: baseball   _____

8. a bet or venture that has only a slight chance of success, an extremely risky undertaking

    Source: horse racing   _____

9. to begin with a severe disadvantage or handicap   ————————

    Source: baseball

10. a person who is prepared to explain, *after* a defeat or disappointment, what went wrong and what should have been done to achieve success. (The expression is ironic.) ————————

    Source: football

11. to start, begin, initiate, or commence   ————————

    Source: football

12. to give up, surrender, or admit defeat   ————————

    Source: boxing

From the list of words and expressions on page 151, choose the item that best completes each of the following sentences. Write it in the space given.

1. "I know that all the polls indicate that we are trailing our opponent," the campaign manager said to the candidate, "but I believe we can beat him at his own game if we ————————."

2. "You may think that I'm down and out," I replied to her comment, "but I am not ready to ———————— just yet."

3. Youngsters who try to enter the work force without the technical or verbal skills needed to handle a job effectively are essentially ————————.

4. "Though my opponent claims to have laid all her cards on the table," the candidate observed wryly, "I have a funny feeling that she still ————————."

5. "I know it's a ————————," the Senator commented, "but this time I think our dark horse may just win."

6. Though he was clearly the ———————— early on in the campaign, a series of political blunders, entirely of his own devising, put him out of contention long before election day rolled around.

7. When the head of the department is out ill, it is up to her assistant to step in and ———————— for her.

8. When the material I needed to finish the project didn't arrive on time, I found myself hopelessly ————————.

9. The televised marathon with which we ———————— this year's charity drive was followed up by a series of smaller, more localized fund-raising events.

10. Others may have felt that the speech was an effective response to the challenges that lay ahead, but I thought the speaker was merely ————————.

11. Long experience has taught me exactly what to expect from that TV series, and last night's episode struck me as being more or less ————————.

12. Since we all know what went wrong in the campaign, I see no reason to subject the matter to a lengthy post-mortem presided over by a bunch of sanctimonious ————————.

Units 4–6

Religious and Philosophical Positions

The word **agnostic,** introduced on page 43, indicates a specific religious or philosophical position. English is rich in such expressions. A few other examples of this type are listed below. All would make good candidates for inclusion in your active vocabulary.

atheist
cynic
empiricist
hedonist
iconoclast
idealist

materialist
monotheist
mystic
pantheist
polytheist
pragmatist

From the list of words given above, choose the item that corresponds to each of the brief definitions below. Write it in the space at the right of the definition.

1. a person who believes that physical matter constitutes the only reality or that physical well-being and worldly possessions form the only good in life _____

        Origin: "matter" (Latin)

2. a person who believes that pleasure is the chief good in life _____

        Origin: "pleasure" (Greek)

3. a person who believes that experience and observation provide the only basis for knowledge _____

        Origin: "experience" (Greek)

4. a person who denies the existence of God _____

        Origin: "without God" (Greek)

5. a person who identifies God with the various forces or workings of nature; a person who believes in or worships all gods _____

        Origin: "all gods" (Greek)

6. a person who sees things in an ideal or perfect form and attempts to realize them, often through visionary or impractical schemes _____

        Origin: "form, model" (Greek)

7. a person who seeks to commune with God or ultimate reality through contemplation or meditation _____

        Origin: "an initiate" (Greek)

8. a person who approaches situations and problems from a purely practical point of view _____

        Origin: "deed, affair" (Greek)

9. a person who believes that there is only one God _____

        Origin: "one god" (Greek)

10. a person who is inclined to doubt or deny the virtuousness, disinterestedness, or honesty of human motives or actions _____

      Origin: "dog" (Greek)

11. a person who opposes the veneration of religious images and destroys them; a person who attacks established beliefs and institutions _____

      Origin: "image-breaker" (Greek)

12. a person who believes in many gods _____

      Origin: "many gods" (Greek)

From the list of words on page 153, choose the item that best completes each of the following sentences. Write it in the space given.

1. Since the pharaoh Akhenaton rejected the numerous gods of Egypt in favor of a single deity, he may have been the world's first _____ .

2. Only a thoroughgoing _____ would seriously argue that everyone has a price.

3. Scientists are essentially _____ because they attempt to base their conclusions solely on observation and experimentation.

4. The writings of such famous _____ as Thomas à Kempis and Richard Rolle are filled with accounts of visions of heaven, angelic visitations, and other transcendental experiences.

5. Some of the early Romantic poets were essentially _____ who imbued the manifold wonders of nature with truly divine attributes.

6. Though the children of Israel believed in one and only one God, the ancient Greeks and Romans were _____ .

7. Since his writings clearly deny the existence of God, I'd classify the author as a(n) _____ , not an agnostic.

8. Someone whose life is so completely concerned with "getting and spending" can only be considered an outright _____ .

9. For a(n) _____ , the sole purpose in life seems to be summed up in the old adage, "Eat, drink, and be merry, for tomorrow you die."

10. At heart she is a(n) _____ who enjoys taking potshots at sacred cows or tweaking the nose of the "Establishment."

11. The world would surely be a great deal nicer if there were really a way to reconcile the dreams of a starry-eyed _____ with the exigencies of practical reality!

12. The new ambassador is a hardheaded _____ , who sees diplomacy as the "art of the possible," rather than an exercise in high-minded futility.

Units 7–9

Our Italian Heritage

Unit 9 includes **dilettante** (page 69), a word borrowed from Italian. Listed below are a number of other Italian words and phrases that are commonly used in present-day English. Each of them would make an attractive addition to your working vocabulary.

a cappella	**prima donna**
cognoscenti	**quarantine**
finale	**scenario**
graffiti	**sotto voce**
imbroglio	**squadron**
libretto	**studio**
manifesto	**tempo**
motto	**torso**

From the list of expressions above, choose the item that corresponds to each of the brief definitions below. Write it in the space at the right of the definition.

1. the trunk of the human body; a statue of the trunk of the human body; anything that is truncated or unfinished _____

> *Original Italian Meaning:* "the body of a statue"

2. a complicated, confused, or difficult situation; an entanglement or predicament _____

> *Original Italian Meaning:* "a tangle"

3. very softly or quietly, so as not to be overheard or attract attention _____

> *Original Italian Meaning:* "under the voice, under one's breath"

4. without any musical accompaniment _____

> *Original Italian Meaning:* "in the manner of [the choir of] a chapel" (where musical instruments were not used)

5. the speed at which a musical composition is played; the characteristic pace of anything _____

> *Original Italian Meaning:* "time"

6. a large military or naval unit; any organized multitude _____

> *Original Italian Meaning:* "a big square [formation of troops]"

7. the lead female singer in an opera; a temperamental person _____

> *Original Italian Meaning:* "first lady"

8. the place or period of isolation (originally forty days) in or during which a person, vehicle, or animal suspected of carrying a disease is detained at a port of entry into a foreign country so as to prevent the disease from spreading to the native populace; any enforced isolation or restriction of free movement; to isolate _____

> *Original Italian Meaning:* "forty days"

9. the printed text of the words to an opera or other musical composition   _____

    Original Italian Meaning: "little book, booklet"

10. an artist's workroom; a photographer's establishment; an establishment where an art or skill is taught; a room or building for motion-picture or radio-TV productions; a one-room apartment   _____

    Original Italian Meaning: "a study"

11. drawings, words, or statements scrawled or drawn on the surfaces of buildings, vehicles, etc.   _____

    Original Italian Meaning: "little scratchings"

12. the end or climax of a theatrical entertainment or other work, especially a musical composition; the end of anything _____

    Original Italian Meaning: "final; end"

13. persons of outstanding knowledge or taste, connoisseurs, experts   _____

    Original Italian Meaning: "those in the know"

14. a public declaration of intentions or principles, especially if these are political in nature   _____

    Original Italian Meaning: "a manifestation"

15. the outline or synopsis of a dramatic or musical work; a screenplay; the outline of a hypothetical situation or chain of events   _____

    Original Italian Meaning: "scenery"

16. a brief sentence or phrase that expresses the purpose, goals, or ideals of some person, group, organization, or institution   _____

    Original Italian Meaning: "a word"

From the list of expressions on page 155, choose the item that best completes each of the following sentences. Write it in the space given.

1. Though many glee clubs and choirs have pianists to accompany them, others sing entirely _____ .

2. The _____ of the United States Marine Corps is "Semper fidelis," which means "Always faithful."

3. Whenever I wish to know exactly what one of the characters in an opera is singing, I consult the _____ .

4. All the famous musical numbers in that famous operetta are reprised in the grand _____ that brings down the final curtain.

5. I couldn't read the map in the subway station because some thoughtless person had scrawled unsightly _____ all over the glass that protected it.

6. Though the exhibition was by no means a hit with the general public, it was well received by the _____ .

7. People who were brought up in sleepy country towns often find it very hard to adjust to the hectic _____ of life in a big city.

8. In *The Communist* _____ , Karl Marx and Friedrich Engels set forth various revolutionary principles that have had a great impact on the course of 20th-century history.

9. The head and limbs of that famous statue were lost in antiquity, and all that now remains is the _____ .

10. The artist was a gregarious individual, whose _____ became a celebrated rendezvous for the greats and near-greats of his time.

11. In her time, she was a famous _____ , whose moving portrayals of the great Verdi and Puccini heroines were justly celebrated all over the world.

12. Antiaircraft fire lit up the night sky as _____ of bombers, flying in tight formation, began to assault the beleaguered city.

13. Tots with such childhood diseases as the measles, mumps, and chicken pox are often _____ to prevent the infection from spreading to their classmates, relatives, or friends.

14. The harder I tried to extricate myself from that _____ , the more deeply entangled in it I seemed to become.

15. I strained to catch the words that the poor wretch hurriedly whispered to me _____ as we passed each other on the way back to our cells.

16. At the meeting, the President's military advisers pointed out that in a "worst-case _____ ," the system might malfunction and leave the entire area defenseless.

Units 10–12

Borrowings from Arabic

In 1095, the First Crusade to recover the Holy Land from the Moslems got under way. Subsequently, eight other crusades were launched. These expeditions brought Europe into contact with the Arabs and Arabic civilization. As a result of these and later contacts, a few Arabic words eventually came into English. One such word, **nadir,** was introduced on page 96. A few other examples are listed below. Many of them you will probably already know. The others would make useful additions to your active vocabulary.

admiral	salaam
alcohol	sherbet
alcove	sofa
algebra	syrup
cipher	tariff
mattress	zenith

From the list of words given above, choose the item that corresponds to each of the brief definitions below. Write it in the space at the right of the definition.

1. any Arabic numeral, including zero; a person or thing without value or influence; a kind of code; a coded message _____

  Original Arabic Meaning: "zero, empty"

2. a duty on imported or exported goods; a system of such duties _____

  Original Arabic Meaning: "information"

3. a partly enclosed recess forming part of a room or garden _____

  Original Arabic Meaning: "the vault"

4. a rectangular pad of heavy cloth stuffed with soft material and used on or as a bed _____

  Original Arabic Meaning: "place where something is thrown"

5. the branch of mathematics that deals with the relations and properties of quantities, usually designated by letters, together with the operations that can be performed on them _____

  Original Arabic Meaning: "the [science of] reuniting (*i.e.,* calculating)"

6. the commander of a navy or a fleet _____

  Original Arabic Meaning: "the commander of [something]"

7. a long upholstered piece of furniture with a back, arms, and cushions and designed to seat several people at once; a couch _____

  Original Arabic Meaning: "raised dais, divan"

8. a thick, sweet, sticky liquid made of sugar, natural or artificial flavorings, and water _____

  Original Arabic Meaning: "a beverage"

9. the highest point above the horizon attained by a celestial body; any summit, pinnacle, or acme   _____

       Original Arabic Meaning: "road over head"

10. a colorless, volatile, and inflammable liquid produced by fermentation and widely used as an intoxicating beverage   _____

       Original Arabic Meaning: "powdered antimony (an element)"

11. a formal salutation or greeting involving a deep bow and the placement of the right hand on the forehead; any respectful greeting; to greet in such a way   _____

       Original Arabic Meaning: "peace [be with you]"

12. a sweet kind of ice made from water or milk and egg white, fruit juice, or gelatin   _____

       Original Arabic Meaning: "a drink"

From the list of words on page 158, choose the item that best completes each of the following sentences. Write it in the space given.

1. A government will sometimes impose stiff _____ on imports in order to protect its own industries from foreign competition.

2. Driving while under the influence of _____ is not just dangerous; it's deadly.

3. High school students usually begin their study of higher mathematics by taking _____ in their freshman year.

4. Horatio Nelson was the English _____ who defeated the emperor Napoleon's fleet at the famous battle of Trafalgar.

5. The night was so hot and humid that not only the sheets on my bed but also the _____ became soaked with perspiration.

6. He plopped himself down on the living room _____ , stuck his feet up on the coffee table, and promptly fell asleep.

7. Despite its name, an "egg cream" is made out of soda water and some kind of vanilla or chocolate _____ .

8. There's nothing quite so refreshing as a little orange, lemon, lime, or raspberry _____ to top off a meal on a hot summer day.

9. My apartment is too small to have a proper bedroom, but I do have a little sleeping _____ right off the kitchen.

10. No one could understand the message found on the captured spy because it was written in _____ .

11. I don't see why I should be expected to _____ before that arrogant lout just because he's a senior and I'm a lowly freshman.

12. After reaching the _____ of its power and influence in the first two centuries of the present era, the Roman Empire began its long, slow descent into oblivion during the third.

Units 13–15

**Our French
Heritage**

English has an extensive store of words and phrases that have been borrowed more or less unchanged from French. One such word, **coup,** was introduced on page 116. Some other examples are listed below. All of them will add to the range and variety of your active vocabulary.

amour propre
avant-garde
boutique
chef d'oeuvre
communiqué
de rigueur
ensemble
entrée

hors d'oeuvre
joie de vivre
nom de plume
par excellence
rapprochement
tête-à-tête
timbre
vis-à-vis

From the list of expressions given above, choose the item that corresponds to each of the brief definitions below. Write it in the space at the right of the definition.

1. a pseudonym used by an author   _____

    Original French Meaning: "pen name"

2. required by the prevailing fashion or custom; socially obligatory, incumbent   _____

    Original French Meaning: "indispensable"

3. the reestablishment of cordial relations, especially between two nations; such a state of affairs   _____

    Original French Meaning: "a bringing together"

4. a group, usually consisting of artists or writers, who develop experimental or innovative techniques; an intelligentsia; of or relating to such a group; ahead of the times   _____

    Original French Meaning: "vanguard"

5. the distinctive tone of a musical instrument or voice   _____

    Original French Meaning: "tone (as of a bell)"

6. an admittance or introduction; privileged access to a place normally inaccessible; the main course of a meal   _____

    Original French Meaning: "entry, entrance"

7. face-to-face with; in relation to; as compared with   _____

    Original French Meaning: "face-to-face"

8. a group composed of complementary elements or parts that contribute to a single effect; music composed for two or more performers   _____

    Original French Meaning: "together"

9. in private, between two persons only; a private conversation between two persons   _____

    Original French Meaning: "head-to-head"

10. a bulletin; an official announcement _____

Original French Meaning: "announcement"

11. a small retail store specializing in fashionable clothing, accessories, or gifts _____

Original French Meaning: "shop"

12. regarded as the best of a kind or the epitome of something _____

Original French Meaning: "by way of preeminence"

13. a masterpiece, outstanding accomplishment _____

Original French Meaning: "masterwork"

14. a keen or carefree enjoyment of life _____

Original French Meaning: "joy of living"

15. self-esteem, self-respect, vanity _____

Original French Meaning: "love of oneself"

16. an appetizer served with cocktails or before a meal _____

Original French Meaning: "outside of [the] work"

From the list of expressions on page 160, choose the item that best completes each of the following sentences. Write it in the space given.

1. "Since the gala benefit is a formal affair," she replied, "I'm afraid that evening dress is _____ ."

2. My friendship with the Senator's daughter gave me _____ to some circles of Washington society that would otherwise have been entirely closed to me.

3. In a brief _____ from the actual field of battle, the general announced his great victory to the President and the nation.

4. It is the _____ of her voice, rather than its size or range, that I find truly extraordinary.

5. Last year, the "mom-and-pop" candy store on the corner was replaced by a chic little _____ that specializes in somewhat pricey designer fashions.

6. President Nixon's 1972 "opening" to China ushered in an era of _____ between the two great superpowers.

7. The large _____ that closes Act II of *Aida* involves not only the principal singers but also several minor characters, the full chorus, and every instrument in the orchestra.

8. Though Leo Tolstoi wrote several remarkable novels, *War and Peace* is without a doubt his _____ .

9. "Sunny" is indeed an apt nickname for a girl whose personality radiates a rare _____ and fascination with life.

10. Of all the famous paladins at King Arthur's legendary court, Sir Galahad is _____ the paragon of knightly virtue and steadfastness.

11. I met her after work for a friendly little _____ in a cozy corner of the local watering hole.

12. During the cocktail party, I kept going back to sample more of the delectable _____ that were spread out in rich profusion on the buffet.

13. That style of painting may have been quite _____ and daring fifty years ago, but by now it is decidedly "old hat."

14. I'm afraid that his rather inflated sense of _____ will not brook the slightest criticism of anything he does, no matter how justified the observation may be.

15. The role the House of Commons plays in shaping the destinies of the British nation, _____ that of Lords, has grown steadily during the course of the country's long history.

16. "Mark Twain," the _____ under which Samuel Clemens published all of his writings, is actually a Mississippi riverboat expression relating to the measurement of water depths.

Working with Parts of Speech

Units 1–3

Adjectives   An *adjective* describes or qualifies a noun. Among the adjectives we encountered in Units 1–3 were *banal, myopic,* and *feckless.* Here are a few more useful adjectives to add to your active vocabulary.

atavistic	**interactive**	**niggling**	**puissant**	**visceral**
foppish	**kinetic**	**protean**	**untrammeled**	

From the list of words above, choose the item that corresponds to each of the brief definitions below. Write the word in the space at the right of the definition and then in the illustrative phrase below it.

1. felt or as if felt by the internal organs, deep; instinctive rather than intellectual, unreasoning; characterized by crude or elemental emotions, earthy   _____

   _____ drives

2. relating to the motion of material things and the forces or energy produced by them; active, lively; dynamic, energized; *(of art)* having mechanical parts that can be set in motion   _____

   _____ energy

3. having the ability to assume different shapes or forms, varying, changeable; displaying great diversity or variety, versatile   _____

   "such _____ shadows so delude our sights" (Marston)

4. unconfined, unhampered, unrestrained   _____

   _____ authority

5. behaving or dressing like a vain and silly person, foolish, silly   _____

   "Fools had ne'er less wit in a year,

   For wise men are grown _____ .
   They know not how their wits to wear,
   Their manners are so apish."   (Shakespeare, *King Lear*)

6. *(of organisms)* having a characteristic or trait typical of an ancestral form; reverting to a past style, manner, outlook, or approach   _____

   _____ influences

7. involving the user's participation; designed to involve the user in some role in order to complete or perform   _____

   a(n) _____ computer program

8. powerful, mighty   _____

   "most _____ Caesar"
        (Shakespeare, *Julius Caesar*)

9. bothersome and persistent in a tiresome or petty way, petty   _____

   _____ complaints

From the list of words on page 163, choose the item that best completes each of the following sentences. Write the word in the space provided.

1. Because the Privy Council exercised immense powers impinging on every aspect of Elizabethan life and politics, its members had to be statesmen of truly _____ abilities.

2. "Carp, carp, carp!" she exclaimed in disgust; "I've had it with the _____ criticisms of professional hairsplitters like you!"

3. "Awake remembrance of these valiant dead,

   And with your _____ arm renew their feats.
   You are their heir; you sit upon their throne;
   The blood and courage that renownéd them

   Runs in your veins; and my thrice-_____ liege
   Is in the very May-morn of his youth,
   Ripe for exploits and mighty enterprises."   (Shakespeare, *Henry V*)

4. One critic called *Who's Afraid of Virginia Woolf* "as emotionally naked and relentlessly _____ a play as our theater has seen in decades."

5. "Oh for a life _____ by such mundane considerations as paying bills, doing the laundry, and going to the dentist," I mused.

6. I think I'd call it a(n) _____ ballet because several times during the performance the dancers waved at the audience and the audience waved back.

7. I've never quite decided whether my passion for foxhunting is the result of my upbringing in the English downs or merely a(n) _____ inheritance from my cave-dwelling ancestors.

8. Modern standards of taste in wearing apparel tend to view men's fashions at the court of Louis XIV as decidedly _____ and effeminate.

9. The old adage that "all roads lead to Rome" reminds us that St. Peter and St. Paul lived in an extraordinarily complex world of which the Eternal City was the _____ center.

Units 4–6

Verbs

Verbs denote actions or states of being—for example, strike and become. In Units 4–6 we encountered several useful verbs, including incarcerate, emend, and travesty. Here are a few more to add to your active vocabulary.

arraign	**extradite**	**gesticulate**	**postulate**	**wrest**
career	**filibuster**	**leach**	**purvey**	

From the list of words above, choose the item that corresponds to each of the brief definitions below. Write the word in the space at the right of the definition and then in the illustrative phrase below it.

1. to use delaying tactics, like endless speechifying, to retard or prevent a legislature from acting; to engage in revolutionary activities in a foreign country   _____

   soldiers of fortune who had _____ in Central America

2. to assume or claim to be true, necessary, or real, hypothesize; to depend upon or start from such a claim or assumption; to demand, claim, require

    might easily _____ such a scenario

3. to call a defendant before a court to answer to a charge; to accuse of wrongdoing

    will be _____ tomorrow

4. to dissolve one substance out of another as the result of the seepage of a liquid through it; to subject to such an action; to remove by or as if by seepage

    _____ nutrients from the soil

5. to sway from side to side, lurch; to cause a boat to lean over on one side

    _____ wildly in the heavy seas

6. to supply, usually as a matter of business; to peddle

    a license to _____ fine wines to the public

7. to make expressive movements of one's arms or hands, especially when speaking

    _____ threateningly at the crowd

8. to pull or force away by a violent twisting action; to gain with difficulty by or as if by force, violence, or labor

    _____ the wallet from my hand

9. to surrender (an alleged criminal) to the authority having jurisdiction to try the case (usually another state or a foreign country) pursuant to the terms of an international treaty or state statute

    quickly _____ the suspect

From the list of words on page 164, choose the item that best completes each of the following sentences. Write the word in the space provided.

1. The sudden death of his beloved wife truly seemed to _____ all meaning from his life, for he was never the same thereafter.

2. Though no formal charges will be brought against the official, he will certainly be

_____ in the court of public opinion, which, no doubt, will not look upon his actions so leniently.

3. By dint of hard and unremitting labor they managed to _____ a living out of the unpromising plot of hardscrabble on which they lived.

4. Though he did not have the votes to defeat the bill outright, the senator was

confident that he could _____ it to death.

5. The speaker had an annoying habit of punctuating her arguments by

_____ vigorously with her index finger.

6. "We could tell you were tipsy," she replied with some disgust, "simply by the way

you _____ down the street, stumbling into passersby and lurching into lampposts as you went."

7. When they learned that the wanted man had fled to Colombia, the authorities in New York initiated steps to _____ him back to the United States for trial.

8. In a society that protects free speech, it is often extremely difficult to "put a lid on" those who use the media to _____ racial hatred.

9. As Samuel Taylor Coleridge once wrote, "In geometry the primary construction is not demonstrated but _____ ."

Units 7–9

Nouns

A *noun* names a person, place, thing, quality, action, or idea. For example, *soldier, kitchen, fork, hope, murder,* and *evolution* are all nouns. In Units 7–9 we encountered a number of useful nouns, including *coterie, paucity,* and *dilettante.* Here are a few more to add to your active vocabulary.

animus	doldrums	imprimatur	mayhem	scintilla
cretin	double entendre	linchpin	physiognomy	

From the list of words above, choose the item that corresponds to each of the brief definitions below. Write the word in the space at the right of the definition and then in the illustrative phrase below it.

1. the facial features as understood to reveal character or inner qualities; the art of discerning these from a person's outward features; any external appearance _____

a student of _____

2. a word or expression that is capable of several interpretations, one of which may be off-color; any ambiguity of language _____

an inadvertent _____

3. listlessness or despondency; a state or period of inactivity, stagnation, or slump _____

an economy in the _____

4. a peg inserted crosswise to lock or hold together a device; anything that serves to hold together all the elements of some complex design _____

insert the _____ into the axle frame

5. a basic attitude or governing spirit, disposition; an unusually prejudiced and spiteful ill will _____

the _____ that led to the Industrial Revolution

6. a spark or flash; a minute amount, a trace, an iota, a jot _____

not a(n) _____ of evidence against them

7. a physically stunted and mentally retarded person; an extremely stupid, vulgar, or insensitive person, a philistine _____

a certifiable _____

8. the willful deprivation of a bodily limb; any willful crippling of the body; any willful damage or violence _____

in the ensuing _____

9. a license to print or publish, especially from a Roman Catholic episcopal authority; approval of a publication from an official censor; any type of sanction or approval; a mark of distinction or honor

      waiting for the _____ from the bishop

From the list of words on page 166, choose the item that best completes each of the following sentences. Write the word in the space provided.

1. As the trial unfolded, it became more and more evident that claims of a monstrous police cover-up of the truth would be the _____ of the defense's case.

2. The dialogue of a typical Restoration "comedy of manners" usually contains more than its fair share of quips, put-downs, _____ , and slightly salacious jokes.

3. Though his manner of speaking was "a little out of fashion," what he said contained more than a(n) _____ of truth in it.

4. Though I could tell nothing from her words, her _____ hinted at a certain dissatisfaction with the arrangement.

5. When Hamlet says that a certain play was "caviare to the general," he means that the play was too well-written to be appreciated by the _____ that made up the bulk of the audience.

6. "The only way you're going to get out of the academic _____ you're in," Dad observed sternly, "is to settle down and *study.*"

7. My boss liked my suggestion so much that he gave it his _____ in an official memo to all departments.

8. The unrelenting _____ which the Lady Ashton harbors against the Ravenswood family does much to precipitate the final catastrophe in Scott's *The Bride of Lammermoor.*

9. When the riot was over, several of the participants were arrested and charged with

      _____ .

Units 10–12

Adjectives

Some English *adjectives* derive from various foreign languages, notably Latin, Greek, and French; others are just plain English. In Units 10–12 we encountered a few such items, including *sporadic, moribund, plaintive,* and *hapless.* Here are a few more to add to your active vocabulary.

avuncular	hoary	pathological	roisterous	sundry
guttural	jocund	preternatural	sentient	

From the list of words above, choose the item that corresponds to each of the brief definitions below. Write the word in the space at the right of the definition and then in the illustrative phrase below it.

1. full of mirth and high spirits, merry

      "in such _____ company" (Wordsworth)

2. existing outside of nature; going beyond what is normal or usual, extraordinary; not explainable by ordinary means, psychic

      _____ phenomena

_____

3. of or relating to an uncle; suggestive of kindliness and geniality

      love, paternal or _____

_____

4. miscellaneous, various

      _____ trading goods

_____

5. engaged in or characteristic of rough and noisy revelry

      _____ companions

_____

6. made in or coming from the throat; low, strange, and unpleasant

      a(n) _____ sort of laugh

_____

7. conscious of or responsive to sense impressions, aware; extremely perceptive of feeling or emotion, especially in others

      not a(n) _____ being

_____

8. gray or white with or as if with age; extremely old, ancient

      _____ with frost

_____

9. relating to the study of disease; deviating from the normal in some structural or functional way as the result or as if as the result of disease; generally changed or caused by disease

      a(n) _____ liar

_____

From the list of words on page 167, choose the item that best completes each of the following sentences. Write the word in the space provided.

1. Those _____ tales of my great-grandfather's Civil War exploits, so lovingly purveyed by his widow, used to fascinate me as a child, but now I prefer stories of more recent vintage.

2. Although he is by no means a blood relation of mine, he has always played a(n)

_____ role in my life, like the part Mr. Jarndyce plays for Esther in *Bleak House.*

3. If one considers the _____ evils to which the body may fall prey, the Biblical "three score and ten" does not seem an unrealistic estimate of the average human life span.

4. Flushed with success in the chase, Bucklaw spends the evening carousing at the

local alehouse in the company of several dozen _____ huntsmen.

5. The low, _____ noises that emanated from his mouth reminded me more of the snarls of some savage beast than of the accents of a civilized human being.

6. The three weird sisters whom Banquo and Macbeth meet on the blasted heath near

Forres certainly appear to possess some _____ knowledge of things yet to come.

7. "No, I don't think asparagus should have the same inalienable rights as humans," I retorted in thorough disbelief, "simply because, though they are alive, they are

hardly _____ ."

8. A(n) _____ fire burned blithely in the grate as the kettle on the hob bubbled and squeaked a merry tune of welcome to the half-frozen traveler.

9. _____ anatomy is the branch of anatomy that concerns itself with the structural changes and other effects disease has on the body.

Units 13–15

Verbs

Verbs can be divided into those that take an object *(transitive verbs)* and those that do not *(intransitive verbs)*. Among the verbs we encountered in Units 13–15 were *affront,* a transitive verb, and *subsist,* an intransitive verb. Here are a few more useful verbs to add to your active vocabulary. (NOTE: Some of these verbs may be used as nouns, *e.g., guffaw.*)

| bemuse | forage | interdict | pontificate | welter |
| confound | guffaw | mulct | transfix | wreak |

From the list of words above, choose the item that corresponds to each of the brief definitions below. Write the word in the space at the right of the definition and then in the illustrative phrase below it.

1. *(intrans.)* to laugh in a loud or boisterous way   _____

_____ at every joke

2. *(trans.)* to punish by a fine; to swindle or defraud of money; to obtain by force, fraud, or theft   _____

_____ them of their life's savings

3. *(trans.)* to inflict (as punishment or vengeance); to give free rein or play to; to bring about, cause   _____

_____ havoc

4. *(trans.)* to confuse or bewilder; to occupy or absorb one's mind or attention   _____

_____ with liquor

5. *(trans.)* to collect or secure (provisions) by searching; to strip of (provisions); *(intrans.)* to wander in search of (provisions); to raid, ravage; to make a search, rummage   _____

"Stood smiling to behold his lion's whelp _____
in blood of French nobility."
(Shakespeare, *Henry V*)

6. *(intrans.)* to act or officiate as chief priest; to speak in a pompous or dogmatic way   _____

hardly the time to _____

7. *(trans.)* to ban or prohibit by law; to forbid formally; to cut off, destroy, or damage by firepower so as to halt an enemy's advance; to halt the advance or activities of   _____

_____ drugs

8. *(trans.)* to pierce through with a pointed object, impale; to hold motionless as if by piercing through

_____

_____ from crown to chaps

9. *(trans.)* to baffle or frustrate; to put to shame, discomfit; to refute; to make someone confused or perplexed, increase the confusion of; to mix up

_____

_____ the critics

10. *(intrans.)* to twist or roll one's body, writhe; to roll and fall about in or as if in waves, toss, wallow; to become deeply sunk, soaked, or involved in; to be in turmoil

_____

"Fallen from his high estate

And _____ing in his blood"
    (Dryden, "Alexander's Feast")

From the list of words on page 169, choose the item that best completes each of the following sentences. Write the word in the space provided.

1. As I was _____ through the game books in search of items I might use in my book on the estate's gardens, I ran across a curious entry relating to a hare Lord Byron had bagged in 1809.

2. Despite the length and complexity of the new play by Tom Stoppard, I was thoroughly _____ by the great actress's riveting performance of the lead character.

3. "I realize this play is a comedy," I said in annoyance to my companion, "but must you _____ so loudly at every line uttered?"

4. "You will never be able to write intelligible English," she observed pointedly, "as long as you _____ the meanings of such words as *militate* and *mitigate* or *humility* and *humidity*."

5. "The embargo we propose is designed to _____ all trade with that nation and so weaken its ability to sponsor acts of international terrorism," the president said.

6. My rival's grandstanding tactics at the board meeting were designed solely to _____ me of my fair share of the glory for the company's success, but fortunately the others present saw through his little game.

7. By the blank or puzzled looks on their faces, I'd say the members of the jury were thoroughly _____ by the obscure technical language in which the so-called "expert" couched his testimony.

8. In Mr. Podsnap, Dickens gives a delightful portrait of the kind of smug, narrow-minded, and pompous old windbag who tends to _____ rather than speak.

9. Oedipus so offended the gods by his actions that they _____ a terrible vengeance on him.

10. "As long as we must _____ in this veritable maelstrom of red tape before a decision can be made," she exclaimed, "nothing will get done!"

Index

The following tabulation lists all the basic words taught in the various units of this workbook, as well as those introduced in the *Vocabulary of Vocabulary, Building with Word Roots, Enhancing Your Vocabulary,* and *Working with Parts of Speech* sections. The number after each item indicates the page on which it is first introduced, but the word may also appear in exercises on later pages.